T. S. ELIOT

Modern Literature Monographs

T. S. ELIOT

Joachim Seyppel

Frederick Ungar Publishing Co.
New York

Published by arrangement with Colloquium Verlag, Berlin.
Translated from the original German, with revisions, by
the author.

Author's Note

Like my study on Faulkner, this contribution to the work of T. S. Eliot deals with a difficult author in brief, concise form. Beyond general interpretations I have tried to draw some parallels between T. S. Eliot on the one hand and continental European writers (especially Rilke), mysticism, and existentialism on the other, because so little has been said in this matter.

This book is for
MARIANNE McDONALD
in gratitude

Acknowledgments

Selected Essays; "The Dry Salvages"; "Choruses from 'The Rock'"; *Notes Towards a Definition of Culture* by T. S. Eliot reprinted by permission of Harcourt Brace Jovanovich, Inc; copyright, 1936, by Harcourt Brace Jovanovich, Inc.; copyright © 1939, 1943, 1949, 1950, 1963, 1964 by T. S. Eliot; copyright, 1967, by Esme Valerie Eliot.

On Poetry and Poets by T. S. Eliot reprinted by permission of Farrar, Straus & Giroux, Inc., copyright © 1943, 1945, 1951, 1954, 1956, 1957 by T. S. Eliot.

Collected Poems 1909-1971; Notes Towards the Definition of Culture; Selected Essays by T. S. Eliot reprinted by permission of Faber and Faber Ltd.

Contents

Contents

Chronology

1888:   Thomas Stearns Eliot born September 26 in St.
           Louis, Missouri.
1906-1910:   Enrolled in Harvard University.
1910-1911:   Enrolled in the Sorbonne.
1911-1914:   Graduate student and assistant in Harvard
           University.
1914:   Visit to Germany, self-exile to England, study in
           Oxford University.
1915:   *The Love Song of J. Alfred Prufrock*; marriage to
           Vivienne Haigh-Wood
1915-1925:   Teacher, bank clerk.
1917:   *Prufrock and Other Observations*; assistant editor
           of *The Egoist* (until 1919).
1920:   *The Sacred Wood; Poems.*
1922:   *The Waste Land.*
1922-1939:   Editor of *The Criterion.*
1925:   *The Hollow Men.*
1926:   Employed by Faber & Gwyer (later Faber &
           Faber); lecturer in Cambridge University; con-
           version to the Anglican High Church.
1927:   Naturalized British subject.
1930:   *Ash Wednesday.*
1932:   *Poems 1909-1925; Selected Essays.*

1933: *Doctor honoris causa* of Columbia University;
       divorced.
1934: *The Rock.*
1935: *Murder in the Cathedral.*
1937: *Doctor honoris causa* of Edinburgh University.
1939: *The Family Reunion; Old Possum's Book of Prac-*
       tical Cats.
1943: *Four Quartets.*
1947: *Doctor honoris causa* of Harvard.
1948: Nobel Prize for Literature.
1950: *The Cocktail Party.*
1952: *The Complete Poems and Plays 1909-1950.*
1954: *The Confidential Clerk;* Goethe Prize, Hamburg,
       Germany.
1957: Married to Esmé Valerie Fletcher; *On Poetry and*
       Poets.
1959: *The Elder Statesman.*
1962: New edition of *The Complete Poems and Plays.*
1965: January 5, T. S. Eliot dies.

1

~~~~~~

Introduction

"In my own experience
of the appreciation of poetry
I have always found
that the less I knew about the poet and his work,
before I began to read it, the better."

T. S. Eliot, *Dante*

The biographer, says T. S. Eliot in his essay "The Frontiers of Criticism," should be "appreciative of the work of the man whose biography he undertakes."[1] Such an approach implies not only sympathy with a poet's themes, but also receptiveness to the form in which he presents them. The problem for a biographer is to make the analysis without destroying the poetic quality of the poem.

Eliot himself said that after reading the analysis of poems that he had known and loved for many years, he was slow to recover his previous feeling for the poems. "It was as if someone had taken a machine to pieces and left me with the task of reassembling the parts."[2] Nonetheless Eliot tended in the beginning of his career as a critic to neglect the content, the philosophy of a poetic work. In his essay of 1927 on "Shakespeare and the Stoicism of Seneca" he states, for instance, that the "poet makes poetry, the metaphysician makes metaphysics, the bee makes honey, the spider secretes' a filament; you can hardly say that any of these agents believes: he merely does."[3] Later, however, he corrected this purely formalistic approach and considered in his criticism the poet's body of thought as a whole. If one were to suggest, for example, that Dante "did not believe the philosophy drawn from Aristotle and the scholastics," then one would be condemning the poems he wrote.[4]

We must take Eliot's work as a whole. If we cannot gain anything from parts of his poetry that reflect only *ennui* we must not immediately turn away. We must try to block off one-sided sympathy or one-sided antipathy and be the go-between for Eliot and his reader. Eliot's *ennui*, to be sure, is not the opposite or the complement of *interest*, but a preparation for much more; *i.e.*, religious contemplation and, in the end, religious conversion. When Eliot remarked on Baudelaire that the Frenchman's *ennui* may be explained psychologically or from the point of view of psychopathology, but that it is also "from the opposite point of view, a true form of *acedia*, arising from the unsuccessful struggle towards the spiritual life,"[5] the underlying thought was that he, Eliot, struggling along the same road, hoped that his own fight would be successful.

One aim of the present work is to throw light on the path that Eliot took from boredom to faith, from doubt and despair toward belief. In addition, this study is meant to prepare the reader to appreciate Eliot's work as such, his poetry as poetry. Eliot's own aim as an essayist was to appreciate art as art and not merely as an "expression of experience." The task is simple or onefold, if we manage to see art as art and as totality of meaning and form, but it becomes twofold if we cannot manage to keep the two aspects in mind simultaneously.

T. S. Eliot was born on September 26, 1888, in St. Louis, Missouri. Mark Twain, too, came from this state, and we know what role the Mississippi River played in Twain's life. In Eliot's case, the role of the river—the Mississippi or another—is veiled. Very late, in the *Four Quartets*, Eliot says:

> I do not know much about gods; but I think that
> the river

Is a strong brown god—sullen, untamed and
                    intractable,
Patient to some degree, at first recognised as a
                    frontier;
Useful, untrustworthy, as a conveyor of commerce. . .
The river is within us. . .[6]

Eliot was quite aware of his compatriot Twain,
and in 1950 wrote a special introduction to an edition of *Huckleberry Finn*. However, if there are any
two writers who represent direct opposites, they are
Mark Twain and T. S. Eliot. In *Huckleberry Finn* and
Tom Sawyer we have folklore and humor, whereas in
The Waste Land there is an extreme esoteric attitude
of despair. Eliot said in an interview in 1930 that his
childhood near the Mississippi meant something to
him that was not exactly communicable; Mark Twain
would have put it similarly, yet each author's literary
exploitation of his Mississippi River experience was
decisively different from that of the other.

Eliot's ancestors belonged to a distinguished New
England family which had originally immigrated from
England. It was the cordwainer Andrew Eliot—not
a common shoemaker but one who worked with special, Spanish leather, "an honest, God-fearing man
from East Coker"—who in the seventeenth century
first settled in Boston. He belonged, together with a
direct ancestor of Nathaniel Hawthorne, to those in
Salem who committed witches to the bonfire.

When the Eliots moved west to St. Louis they
took great care not to disrupt their connections with
New England. Their pride in stemming from the old-

est American aristocracy and in coming from the cradle of American culture expanded in direct proportion to their geographical distance from that cradle. Grandfather Eliot founded Washington University in St. Louis. Father Eliot was a businessman. Mother Eliot showed literary ambitions; she wrote a biography of her father-in-law as well as a dramatic poem on Savonarola, the Italian monk who, two hundred years before the Salem "witches," was burned for heresy.

The Eliots, being liberally and scientifically orientated, were members of the Unitarian Church, which had its headquarters in Boston and Harvard. Out of this religious affiliation there arose for T. S. Eliot the second "imponderability" of his life, after the Mississippi; he called it the "Boston doubt." This doubt took the form of a skepticism difficult to communicate to those not born with it.

Eliot spent most of his childhood and youth in St. Louis. Around 1890, St. Louis had some fewer than half a million inhabitants. The Mississippi as a "conveyor of commerce" was losing more and more ground to the railroads at that time; the door to the West, formerly "wild," and the frontier became part of the new technology. The boredom of civilization began to replace the old adventures—instead of cowboys there were gangsters; instead of the fight for survival in nature there was the fight for survival in business. Of heroic times there remained at most memories. The young man T. S. Eliot did not go West; he stayed on the Mississippi and later went back East.

During Eliot's youth, St. Louis became one of the industrial centers of the Middle West. (The make-up of society in such a town was satirically described soon thereafter by a novelist of Eliot's own generation, Sinclair Lewis, who pictured in *Babbitt* the archetype of the American provincial of that time.) In addition to the urban industrialization and provincialism to which young Eliot was exposed, there was a third important force in his life, religious tradition. Mrs. Eliot was attracted by Church enthusiasm, reform ideas, and fanaticism, and we may imagine the atmosphere of the house as religiously strict, despite the moderating influence of Unitarianism. Besides, there was the influence of an Irish governess of whom young Thomas was quite fond; it was she who first brought him into close contact with Catholicism, and who took him to Catholic mass. Thus the influences intermingled. When, in 1955, the poet spoke about Goethe, he confessed—in antithesis to the German writer—to a "Catholic cast of mind, a Calvinistic heritage, and a Puritanical temperament."[7]

In St. Louis Eliot attended the Smith Academy, from 1898 until 1905. Latin and Greek, French and German, ancient and modern history, and mathematics were his major subjects. He was an ardent reader. Byron impressed him considerably; he wrote an epic poem in Byron's manner. First attempts at poetry were printed in the *Smith Academy Record*.

Eliot's only chances to escape the boredom of St. Louis were summer vacations on the Atlantic coast of Massachusetts. In 1905 and 1906 he enrolled in

Milton Academy, seven miles south of Boston. In 1906 he enrolled in Harvard University and was more intensely exposed to American literary tradition; but here, too, European influences—Shakespeare, Goethe, Dante—made themselves strongly felt. Young T. S. Eliot had come from the realm of Middle West provincialism to the American intellectual metropolis. He met, among others, George Santayana, the Ibero-American philosopher and poet, and Irving Babbitt, most prominent among Romanists and literary historians; both influenced him profoundly. (In 1927, in his review of Irving Babbitt's book *Democracy and Leadership*, he draws the line between gratitude and criticism or refutation of his former teacher.) In 1907 William James held his last lecture course in Harvard, an introduction to philosophy which drew into his lecture hall the entire studentry interested in philosophy and the new pragmatism. Eliot, however, already showed a greater inclination toward the nonpragmatic European thinking of the age.

Between 1907 and 1910 Eliot published his first nine mature poems in the *Harvard Advocate*, the journal of Harvard University students; from 1909 until 1910 he was its editor and thus received a practical apprenticeship in the publishing field. The poet and the critic slowly emerged. Social connections had helped him on, and his sharp intelligence was clearly recognized. Still missing were the decisive contacts with new literary currents, the decisive inspiration by an exciting example of modern poetry, the step toward avant-garde literature. In 1908 Eliot read Arthur Symons' *The Symbolist Movement in Literature.* As he later confessed it opened his eyes; it was one of those books that determined his career. It directed his attention to Laforgue and Rimbaud, Verlaine and Corbière. The French symbolists became his prototypes. Among those first nine poems for the *Harvard Advocate* were "Nocturne," "Humoresque," and "Spleen"; in 1909 and 1910 he wrote "Conversation Gallante," "Portrait of a Lady," and two "Preludes." The titles and associations alone indicate the French influence. In 1911 Eliot wrote "Rhapsody on a Windy Night" and *"La Figlia che Piange,"* and later he even composed poems in the French language.

Fellow students describe Eliot as a young man who, apart from his accent, was quite like an Englishman. He smoked a pipe, liked to be alone, avoided American slang, and dressed with the studied carelessness of a dandy. Thus we can observe an early twofold inclination toward Europe, in intellect to the French, in disposition to the English. His later conversion to a true European was foreshadowed in Boston-Cambridge. The Londoner from St. Louis was in the making.

In 1909 he graduated. As laureate of his class he wrote an ode which was published in the *Harvard Advocate* a year later. From 1909 until 1910 he studied philosophy at the Harvard Graduate School and received his Master of Arts degree. The intellectual horizon of T. S. Eliot, now twenty-two, still more or less limited by and to Boston and Harvard, by and to the United States, was bound to expand. For someone who, like Eliot, was yearning for intellectual adventures, the United States must look quite provincial. A trip abroad led him to France. Here at the Sorbonne in Paris, he studied philosophy and French literature from 1910 until 1911. Philosophy was still his major subject; it was "in him," as he said. He attended lectures by Henri Bergson and passed through a temporary "conversion" to Bergsonism; over an hour before Bergson's lectures began the American in Paris appeared in the crowded lecture hall in order to get a seat. The immediate contact with France, home of symbolism, made a lasting impression on him. Thirty-four years later he remembers: "*Je crois que c'était une bonne fortune exceptionelle, pour un adolescent, de découvrir Paris en l'an 1910. . .*" France, for him, was simply *poetry.*

The Boston of 1911 must have been disillusioning for the returning Eliot. Now neither old St. Louis nor the even older Mississippi, neither New England nor Harvard could charm the young European traveler. And he did not stay long. At first he took up studies in Sanskrit and in the humanities, and taught as 'an assistant in Harvard's Department of Philosophy. Under Josiah Royce (a student of Lotze in Göttingen, Germany), William James, and Charles Peirce, he took up the study of modern pragmatism. He was especially interested in the philosophy of Bradley and in the phenomenologists Meinong and Husserl; Aristotle also belonged to his field of research, which thus spanned both the most ancient and the most modern trends. Eliot began to write his dissertation on F. H.

Bradley's and Meinong's theories on objects of knowledge.

One must neither put Eliot's occupation with philosophy aside as a minor thing, nor underestimate his encounter with such men as Bertrand Russell, in Boston in the year 1914. Philosophy and philosophers continued to play an important role in his poetry and life, and his entire work is penetrated by a philosophical turn of mind that sometimes even surpasses the purely poetical. His inclination to the English metaphysical poets of the seventeenth century, especially John Donne, is evidence of his interest in ideas and abstractions. Bradley taught that "the ultimate fact is experience which means indissoluble unity with the perceived"; this teaching led directly to Meinong's *Gegenstandstheorie* (theory of objects), which emphasized that an object is something which stands before us, upon which the mind can direct itself, a correlation to all intentional acts, to all things that can be "meant" or intended, as *e.g.* even a square circle (which does not exist outside of "intention" or an idea). This is a philosophy which gives mind, or consciousness, the priority over being (the objective). With this attempt to found a new system of logical idealism—untouched by objective reality—the poet Eliot must have been pleased; for on such a basis of purely imaginative thinking the poet won the right to absolute freedom of composition. Even though the poet does not really *need* such a theory or philosophy, Eliot was at least satisfied to have encountered ideas which came close to his own. The poet Eliot's later neglect of the objec-

tive realities of time and space and the so-called "natural truths" was the poetic evaluation and realization
of a philosophical theory. Or rather: philosophy was
confirmed by poetry.

For the situation of modern poetry it is, in any
case, significant that Eliot was influenced by some of
the twentieth century's most important thinkers. James
in the United States, Bergson in France, Bradley in
England, Meinong in the German-speaking parts of
Europe, and above all Husserl, all left their mark on
him. The line that leads from Husserl to Heidegger
was drawn by Eliot in his poetry, especially by his
subjectively or existentially colored concept of time.

American and English literature of Eliot's time
was for a beginner like him quite "useless," as he said
himself; it was dominated by the aging Henry James
(brother of the philosopher William James at Harvard) and his psychological novels from which, however, Eliot could learn at least "something," as he once
remarked. Melville had died in 1891, his real importance still undiscovered. Walt Whitman, whose work
Eliot did not like, had died in 1892. Up to the first
publications of Ezra Pound, the new force, there was a
literary void. A literary tradition of the drama did not,
at that time, exist in the United States. Literature of
the United States in general was slow in the making.
Robert Frost was born in 1875, Carl Sandburg in 1878,
Wallace Stevens in 1879, William Carlos Williams in
1883, Ezra Pound in 1885. For Eliot the years from
1900 until 1914 were, as far as literature is concerned,
a "complete vacuum." By comparison, contemporary

philosophy was alive and offered Eliot at least the cause to move intellectually into new directions. The beginning of pragmatism and of new European philosophical schools (life-philosophy, Bergsonism, phenomenology) helped the young poet to gain new realms of being. And vice versa, new European schools of literature (Proust, Rilke, Yeats, Joyce) discovered new realms of the psyche which enlarged the philosophical view of human existence.

One generation later, Eliot cast a glance back; the poet, fifty-two years of age, reevaluates his youth. In 1940, speaking about Yeats in the Abbey Theatre in Dublin to Friends of the Irish Academy, he says:

When I was a young man at the university, in America, just beginning to write verse, Yeats was already a considerable figure in the world of poetry, and his early period was well defined. I cannot remember that his poetry at that stage made any deep impression upon me. A very young man, who is himself stirred to write, is not primarily critical or even widely appreciative. He is looking for masters who will elicit his consciousness of what he wants to say himself, of the kind of poetry that is in him to write. The taste of an adolescent writer is intense, but narrow: it is determined by personal needs. The kind of poetry that I needed, to teach me the use of my own voice, did not exist in English at all; it was only to be found in French.[8]

Later in the same lecture, he says that in his own time of youth "there seemed to be no immediate great powers of poetry either to help or to hinder, either to learn from or to rebel against."[9] Only in philosophy and in French literature had he found inspiration.

I refer to the tradition which starts with Baudelaire, and culminates in Paul Valéry. I venture to say that without this French tradition the work of three poets in other languages—and three very different from each other—I refer to W. B. Yeats, to Rainer Maria Rilke, and, if I may, to myself—would hardly be conceivable. And, so complicated are these literary influences, we must remember that this French movement itself owed a good deal to an American of Irish extraction: Edgar Allan Poe.[10]

Irish extraction, we may add, is not only important because of Yeats or Poe in particular, but also because of the generally strong influence of Irish literature on American authors, both from the point of view of personal contacts—as in Eliot's own youth—and of literary media and language. Eliot even goes so far as to say that "largely through his influence on three French poets of three successive generations," Poe "may be considered European."[11] Eliot may have held this extreme opinion because he himself, the American expatriate from St. Louis, felt as European as any Englishman; or at least tried to, whether successfully or not. This extreme judgment also may be understood as a late justification or rationalization of his quitting the United States.

In any case, Eliot's turning to philosophy and to philosophers who were at home in Europe, his attraction to French poetry, were his farewell to an America that, for him, seemed to have passed directly from the primitivity of the pioneer days to the decadence of industrialized society. St. Louis or Boston, even Harvard, despite all the refinements of technology and civilization, were only a world of boredom

—by no means a "new" world with hope for the future, which, according to the doubtful dictum of the "American philosopher" John Dewey, was to present to waiting mankind a new culture. Young T. S. Eliot rather hoped to experience, and possibly to help to create, a young literature in "old" Europe. The leap to Paris —a true, existential, Kierkegaardian leap—had strengthened this belief in him; his return to Cambridge, USA, was but the preparation for his second trip abroad. Long before the migration of the "lost generation" to Europe, before Hemingway, MacLeish, and Gertrude Stein, T. S. Eliot returned whence his forefathers had come. Reminiscences of his youth near the Mississippi River or the Atlantic Coast were to be the dearer, the more significant for him *over there.*

2

Prufrock

The new literary idiom that T. S. Eliot had discovered for himself while still in America was to undergo elaboration in Europe. In 1914 he received a travel grant that carried him across the Atlantic. During his relatively short stay in Germany, another philosopher exerted a strong influence on him, Rudolf Eucken in Jena. When World War I broke out Eliot went to England and registered at Merton College of Oxford University. He occupied himself further with German philosophy, and also with Greek thought, above all with Aristotle.

In 1915 for the first time a poem by Eliot was published in an important literary journal: "The Love Song of J. Alfred Prufrock," in *Poetry*. This journal, "A Magazine of Verse," had been founded by Harriet Monroe for the purpose of furthering modern poetry. Its correspondent from 1912 to 1919 was Ezra Pound, who met Eliot in September 1915 and persuaded him to let him have "Prufrock."

Pound had been in Europe since 1908, at first around the Mediterranean, later in England until 1920. In 1913 Pound gathered young insurgents around him and with the help of their poetic endeavors illustrated the principles of "Imagism." The Imagists wanted: to use the common speech but always the "exact" word; to create new rhythms as expression of new moods for the purpose of which "free verse" was most suited; to have absolute freedom in their choice of subject matter; to set an "image" instead of empty generalities; to create a poetry which was "hard and sane," "nearer the bone," "austere, direct,

free from emotional slither"; and to achieve concentration upon the essentials.[12]

These theses were partly quite acceptable and
natural, even for conservatives, and partly—for instance
in the use of common speech—quite provocative and
revolutionary. However, the Imagists often enough
violated their own rules. Pound very soon disengaged
himself from the group (to which, among others, D. H.
Lawrence and H.D., alias Hilda Doolittle, belonged);
yet his influence upon Eliot remained decisive. To no
other American does Eliot refer so often as to Ezra
Pound; he calls him the "greatest disciple" of Browning.[13] The direct personal contact between the two
lasted until 1921 when Pound moved to Paris, and was
continued in various ways far beyond that year.

"The Love Song of J. Alfred Prufrock" was in
Pound's hands for six months before he persuaded
Harriet Monroe to publish the poem in *Poetry*. Eliot
received a fee of eight guineas for the publication.
The literary echo was weak; today these one hundred
and thirty lines belong to the "classical" verses of modern poetry. Eliot had begun the poem in 1910 and
finished it in 1911, when he was visiting Munich from
Paris. The poem of the nineteenth century was out-
dated with "Prufrock." To be sure, love was its subject
matter—as love had always been poetry's subject—but
this love was without any "romantic" touch, without
any illusion. Now the modern city, disillusionment, disappointment, stood in the foreground. If eros prevails,
then only ironically—or from a melancholy point of
view, out of nostalgia that remembered, desperately,

what Tristan and Isolde or Romeo and Juliet once had
meant. The beginning lines may still sound somewhat
"romantic":

> Let us go then, you and I,
> When the evening is spread out against the sky

The third line destroys the idyll.

> Like a patient etherised upon a table;

Evening, sky, a certain atmospheric value—all this may
have been, in 1915, familiar to the poetry-loving
reader; but the invasion, in verse, of such things as
disease, medical science, and operation moves us, immediately and forcefully, into the present age with its
typical conflicts. This is the age of traffic accidents in
the city, of the ambulance, of hospitals, of new and
progressive misery. This combination of traditional
poetry-substance (evening, sky) and technical-age
experiences was present in European poetry at the
same time (Rilke's *Malte Laurids Brigge* and Gottfried Benn's "Morgue" and "Krebsbaracke," the bar-
racks of cancer). T. S. Eliot was not alone in his poetic
experiments.

   In deserted streets, in one-night cheap hotels, and
in "sawdust restaurants with oyster-shells," Prufrock's
desire for love is realized. Yet in all *ennui,* in boredom,
in disgust there is a sentimental mood which brings
the poem close to us, acoustically as well as emotion-
ally. Eliot here proves himself a master of the creation
of lyrical atmosphere. It is mastership, while present-
ing daily routine and misery, still to write in a melody

which pleases us despite its negative accompanying
words; and it is, again, this mastership which characterizes Eliot and differentiates him from poets who
describe social evils merely naturalistically. Perhaps
it is the English language itself which here proves to
have a quality that excels in the reflection of both
ennui and melancholy—a quality that very often is
missing in the translations of Eliot's works. Eliot himself is quite aware of the poetic merits of the English language.

It has often been claimed that English, of all the languages of modern Europe, is the richest for the purpose of
writing poetry. I think that this claim is justified. But
please notice that when I say "richest for the purpose of
writing poetry" I have been careful in my words: I do not
mean that England has produced the greatest poets, or the
greatest amount of great poetry. That is another question
altogether. There are as great poets in other languages:
Dante is certainly greater than Milton, and at least as great
as Shakespeare. And even for the quantity of great poetry,
I am not concerned to maintain that England has produced
more. I simply say that the English language is the most
remarkable medium for the poet to play with. It has the
largest vocabulary: so large, that the command of it by
any one poet seems meagre in comparison with its total
wealth. But this is not the reason why it is the richest language for poetry: it is only a consequence of the real reason. This reason, in my opinion, is the variety of the elements of which English is made up. . . . But I am not
thinking, in all this history, only of the Words, I am
thinking, for poetry, primarily of the Rhythms . . . and
the richness of the English language for poetry is first of
all in its variety of metrical elements . . . the English
language enjoys constant possibilities of refreshment from

its several centres: apart from the vocabulary, poems by
Englishmen, Welshmen, Scots and Irishmen, all written in
English, continue to show differences in their Music.[14]

But, vice versa, the "truly great poet makes his language a great language."[15]

Even if Eliot overestimates English poetry (he
speaks of England as the land of poetry, of Italy and
France as the lands of painting, and of Germany as
that of music), one can agree with him as to the me-
lodic qualities of modern English verse. Its melody is
softer, more elegiac, and less prosaic than is often perceived. The beginning of "Prufrock" is proof of that.

Vis-à-vis Prufrock's meager mediocrity there are,
dissonantly and ironically, the women who talk of Mi-
chelangelo. But this artistic and intellectual giant of
Italian arts is, naturally, far away. We are in Boston
—or London or Paris—of the early twentieth century, in
the world of modern Philistines. Prufrock strikes us as
their symbol. Above all hovers the yellow fog, the yellow smoke, the smog, and there are the pools and the
soot of their chimneys. The month is October—but
nothing here of that October which Thomas Wolfe
describes as the most beautiful, and most tragic,
month of the year. It is the October of our slums.
Only night can save us, and sleep. Time passes by—
and murder, birth, work, indecisions, "visions and
revisions," and the "taking of a toast and tea," the
usual. Toast and tea are the features of general and
universal indifference, of the dominating routine of
life, of tediousness, of social rites to which man clings
as his last resort, cold snobbery of a civilization me-

chanically divided into the twenty-four-hour system. The concept of time evolves as one of the most important and essential problems in the work of Eliot. What can one do? One grows old, one's hair is growing thin, the necktie is "rich," yet modest, and people will say that one's arms and legs are thin . . .

> Do I dare
> Disturb the universe?

Boredom remains, old and well-known things remain, and disappointment remains. There is the useless wish

> I should have been a pair of ragged claws
> Scuttling across the floors of silent seas.

The phrasing "I should have been" is the expression of the wish toward some form of transformation —a wish which, at about the same time, Kafka expressed in *The Metamorphosis* and Gottfried Benn in his "Gesänge" ("O that we were our ancestors / a lump of slime in a warm moor"—"A leaf of sea-weed or a dune-hill / shaped by the wind and heavy toward the bottom. / Even the head of a dragon-fly, the wing of a sea-gull / were too much and suffer too much"). One wishes to be changed into claws, into something elementary and primitive, not into complicated organisms with brains; brainless, simple life is so much easier, and so far removed from mind and intellect with their problems. Man is "fed up with his forehead" (Benn). Man must not ask ("Prufrock"), not dare, not begin. Everything hopeless, life as well as art. "Prufrock" ends with the line:

> and we drown.

The "desire for decline," the "displeasure in civilization" (Spengler, Freud) of the beginning of the twentieth century determine T. S. Eliot's early poetry. When
Eliot moved to England, he was still a relatively young
man who had in early maturity and early pessimism
become convinced of the fragility of his era and culture; but at the same time he was convinced of his
own intelligence and talent. At the age of twenty-
seven he was ready to, and did, challenge society and
its exponents.

In 1916 Henry James died, the American in London, representative of a generation that was sensitive
but still, as a whole, comparatively square-minded and
self-centered. With Henry James a piece of New England, of Boston and Harvard, had been transplanted
back to England. Eliot at that time did not quite
know whether he should continue the Henry James
line of American-English literary tradition or whether
he should turn completely to philosophy. In any case,
in 1916 he finished his dissertation *Experience and the
Objects of Knowledge in the Philosophy of F. H. Bradley.* Would the young man now continue the Anglo-
Saxon trend of empirical philosophy, or would he
rather turn to the more universal tradition of poetic
metaphysics (from Donne to Verlaine)? The fate of
the dissertation itself gives an answer to these questions; it remained unpublished. It was accepted by
the Graduate School of Harvard University because it
was, as Eliot himself said ironically, quite unreadable;
but he never applied officially for the doctorate. With
Eliot's refusal to crown his academic career with a

doctor's cap two things became obvious: his hesitation
to accept unconditionally traditional methods of ab-
stract thinking, and his final breach with the American
mother-country. (The manuscript of the dissertation
can today be read in the Houghton Library of Harvard
University.)

The question remained as to how Eliot would fit
into his age and society. Concretely speaking, what
job would he take? Eliot's ideal was something that
George Santayana had exemplified in Cambridge,
Massachusetts; the personal union of professor and
poet, of critic and writer. However, the way toward
such a goal was infinitely more difficult for him. Since
1915 he had been married to the daughter of the
painter Charles Haigh-Wood. Until 1917 he earned his
livelihood as teacher at the High Wycombe Grammar
School near London, teaching languages, mathematics,
art, swimming, geography, history, and baseball (sar-
castically, Eliot later enumerates all these subjects).
Then he worked as a clerk in the Colonial Department
of Lloyd's Bank until 1925; these years, he says, were
quite satisfactory. He received laudations for the
weekly summaries of reports on commerce and the
contributions on foreign trade that he wrote for
Lloyd's Bank Economic Review.

In 1917, *Prufrock and Other Observations* was
published as a book. The volume contained poems
from his student years, some of which had been
printed in the *Harvard Advocate*, some not previously
published. Among "Other Observations," in poetic
form, is "Portrait of a Lady." The title goes back, in-

tentionally or not, to the title of Henry James's novel of 1881 as well as to that of Pound's poem *"Portrait d'une femme."* Pound's poem is as much suggestion as Eliot's is execution. There we hear of gossip, boredom, the unreality of that lady, here we hear of life without friendship, of Paris in the spring or the empty snobbery of that lady. Again, with tea and conversation, time passes, the fog of December comes, lilacs in April, violin music in August, nights of October, the circle closes, and if the lady should die "some afternoon"—"should I have the right to smile?"

In "Preludes" we encounter impressions that are now stylistically familiar to the reader of T. S. Eliot; impressions of seasons, time of day, streets, winter, evening, passageways, steak smells, smoke, rain, leaves, newspapers, cab-horses, lamps. . . . Early morning is not, essentially, different from other times of day, the same monotony reigns, only at another hour—furnished rooms in a dim dawn. The soul is constituted of a "thousand sordid images." Or it is "stretched tight across the skies / That fade behind a city block."

> I am moved by fancies that are curled
> Around these images, and cling:
> The notion of some infinitely gentle
> Infinitely suffering thing.

"Rhapsody on a Windy Night" repeats such images of the futility of being, the vanity of action, the meaninglessness of human existence. Four o'clock in the morning as the last stage of the night:

> "The bed is open; the tooth-brush hangs on the wall,
> Put your shoes at the door, sleep, prepare for life."
> The last twist of the knife.

The hourglass runs on. "Morning at the Window" leaves us with little more than an "aimless smile that hovers in the air / And vanishes along the level of the roofs." What, after all, is life? Where can we discover the ideals of modern society? Why should I dare to move on? *The Boston Evening Transcript* is our hope when work is done, but its readers only "Sway in the wind like a field of ripe corn." After the death of "Aunt Helen" in the poem with that title life goes on as if nothing had happened (or: the undertaker is aware "that this sort of thing had occurred before"), and the "Dresden clock continued ticking on the mantelpiece." What are our values? Whom do we love, and who loves us? The emptiness of what we experience is shown in "Cousin Nancy" who "smoked / And danced all the modern dances" and whose "aunts were not quite sure how they felt about it, / But they knew that it was modern." *Values*? Laws? Things of convention and history which have no actual bearing upon our time. All that the poet remembers of dowager Mrs. Phlaccus and Professor and Mrs. Channing-Cheetah are "a slice of lemon, and a bitten macaroon" (in the poem "Mr. Apollinax," a satirical piece on the United States). "Fragments of the afternoon might be collected" if "the shaking of her breasts could be stopped," breasts of a woman who is present at a garden tea party, and the poet concentrated his attention "with careful subtlety to this end," we read in the prose piece "Hysteria" that is strewn in among the poems. *Vacuity* is the key word around which the poem "Conversation Galante" is built ("music which we seize / To body forth our own vacuity"). Emptiness, the void of parties, so-called freedom of mental exertion, idleness, even lack of intelligence and outright stupidity, in the end absolute nothingness, that is all that remains from talk and chatter. Whatever you do—

> But weave, weave the sunlight in your hair.
> (*"La Figlia Che Piange"*)

From 1917 to 1919 Eliot was assistant editor of the Imagist journal *The Egoist* and contributor to the journal *Athenaeum.* The bank clerk used the little spare time he had for literary endeavors. However, the age was not favorably disposed to such "extravagancies." The First World War entered into its decisive stage. In 1918 Eliot volunteered for the United States Navy, but was rejected because of poor health.

Speaking in 1940 about this period, Eliot said: "from 1919 on . . . my own course of evolution was already determined."[16] The poet, so it seemed to him about twenty years later, had won out over the philosopher. In 1919 he published seven pieces of his work in *Poems*; in the volume *Ara Vos Prec* of 1920 they were put together with other new works. The volume *Poems*, significantly enough, begins with "Gerontion" (Greek *geronten*—the old ones). Eliot, thirty years old, wrote:

> Here I am, an old man in a dry month. . .

The "old man" talks about neither having been "at the hot gates" nor having fought "in the warm rain" or "knee deep in the salt marsh." Was this the reaction of a man who had been rejected by the military and therefore had not been in the war? Was this part of the feeling of the "lost generation"? Was this the feeling of "guilt," of inferiority in face of the fact that a friend of his Parisian time had been killed in action in 1915 with the Dardanelles expedition? (To this friend he dedicated *Prufrock and Other Observations*; "For Jean Verdenal, 1889-1915, *mort aux Dardanelles*.*") In any case, the old sentiments form part of the new poetry. His house is "decayed." A woman "keeps the kitchen, makes tea." Everyday life of modern Everyman rules as before the war—not even the *war* has changed anything. An old man, a "dull head among windy spaces." Disillusionment. Awareness of futility, even more so after a war that had brought neither peace nor revolution against the endless circle of arms-making and armistice but instead only the germs of the next war to follow soon. History guides us "by vanities."

> After such knowledge, what forgiveness?
> . . . .
>   Think
> Neither fear nor courage saves us. Unnatural vices
> Are fathered by our heroism. Virtues
> Are forced upon us by our impudent crimes.

The postwar philosophy of Nihilism is apparent. Even earlier in the motto to "Gerontion" Eliot warned

> Thou hast nor youth nor age
> But as it were an after dinner sleep
> Dreaming of both.

And the end of the poem states flatly there are but

> Thoughts of a dry brain in a dry season.

All that seems to remain, at this moment, are age, se-
nility, sterility, and decline. Thoughts of a man who is
but thirty.

The Eliot we see on the cover of *The Complete Poems and Plays 1909-1950*,[17] face glib and full
of furrows, tired yet forcing a smile, hair carefully
parted and wet, in the suit of the gentleman complete
with handkerchief, reflects the feeling of the "old man"
of "Gerontion" overpowered by worried hopelessness,
by preoccupation with an unavoidable fate, torn by
useless pedantry in the face of chaos. It is a polite,
obliging, tactful face, concerned with human problems, seeming to look both toward the reader and into
himself. A face, however, looking actually at nothing,
not at an object and not even at himself. The face of a
profound Boston skeptic. It seems to ask: *Well?* What
do *you* think? And seems to nod and to resign itself.
This face knows sympathy—but salvation? It is no
longer the face of the elegant young man of about
thirty that can be seen in a book on the history of
American literature published ten years earlier, in
1952.[18]

"Burbank with a Baedeker: Bleistein with a Cigar"
—the poem is a document of the age of travel agencies

and of tourists and snobs. The fact that both Burbank and Bleistein happened to have picked Venice as their destination belongs to the tradition of Shakespeare, Byron, Robert Browning (highly thought of by Eliot), Ruskin, Oscar Wilde, and Ezra Pound. Pound published his first opus there (*A Lume Spento*, 1908). Hemingway returned there after the Second World War. French and German literature have often found their settings there. And Burbank with the Baedeker and Bleistein with a cigar.

Around 1920, Eliot had at last to break with the Romantic tradition, hardly a decade after Thomas Mann's *Death in Venice*. His "poem," a poem by virtue of its rhymes, is prosaic and sarcastic. The famous sunrise over the Adriatic Sea which Browning described shortly before his death, which Thomas Mann's death-bound traveler Aschenbach and even Hemingway's Colonel Cantwell admire, is sketched only briefly by Eliot.

> The horses, under the axletree
>   Beat up the dawn from Istria
> With even feet.

More important, for Eliot, are Bleistein's "saggy bending of the knees," his visit to the Rialto ("once"), the rats "underneath the piles." The "Chicago Semite Viennese" figures as the symbol of the fugitive without roots, of forlornness, of bondage to strange and alienating powers like money. This fugitive is not even, like the Romantics, "home-sick," as he has no home. He represents beyond that the most conspicuous example of the modern business-civilization in which we all have become the "hollow men."

The word "waste," which later became part of Eliot's most famous poem, appears in the first line of "Sweeney Erect." The scene shows Sweeney, a dubious lover, shaving. He appears as the opposite of the heroes of Greek myths, and of Emerson's hero whose "lengthened shadow" is history. (Emerson, of course, "had not seen the silhouette / Of Sweeney in the sun.") Sweeney has nothing at all of the hero; he is but part of the shapeless masses.

Certain poems in the French language that follow must be considered experiments that grew out of the strong influence that French poets had on T. S. Eliot. They are comparable to the verses of Ezra Pound, which contain elements of many languages. With Eliot and Pound a large-scale attempt is made to mobilize world literature for the modern poetic laboratory. Besides foreign language poems and verses with numerous quotations we must mention the mottoes which Eliot takes from Italian, Latin, Ancient French, and Greek. They haven't the function of an introduction to the contents of the poem; rather, they are in dialectical contrast to that contents. The element of "Romantic irony" which once stood at the end of a poem (*e. g.* with Heinrich Heine, on whom Pound composed a wonderful epitaph) is now to be found at the beginning, and it aims a priori at the destruction of any possible Romantic illusion.

"A Cooking Egg" begins with an Ancient French motto. *"Mélange Adultère de Tout"* strews in, somewhat out of place—or perhaps ironically—German words such as *"Emporheben"* which rhyme with *"Bergsteigleben"*; "The Hippopotamus" quotes S. Ignatii Ad Trallianos and the Bible, and begins:

> The broad-backed hippopotamus
> Rests on his belly in the mud;
> Although he seems so firm to us
> He is merely flesh and blood.

The aim of the poem is to point out certain deficiencies in a clerical life that are not in keeping with true Biblical teaching. The whole poem is pure irony. In a manner somewhat similar to that of a nursery rhyme, certain unrelated lines aim at the reader's enlightenment.

> Flesh and blood is weak and frail,
> Susceptible to nervous shock;
> While the True Church can never fail
> For it is based upon a rock.
> The hippo's feeble steps may err
> In compassing material ends,
> While the True Church need never stir
> To gather in its dividends.

But in the end, the hippopotamus "shall be washed as white as snow" and ascend to heaven, whereas the "True Church remains below."

Nothing is felt here of the mood upon which, almost a decade later, T. S. Eliot based his conversion to the Anglican High Church, unless the poem is interpreted as belonging to that studied "Satanism" of Baudelaire[19] which is supposed to lead to Christianity "through the back door." The poem "Whispers of

Immortality" is, like "The Hippopotamus," far removed from any feeling of positive religiousness. If
death be predominant in our lives, we only "crawl"
between "dry ribs" in order to "keep our metaphysics
warm." Even *death*, then, means nothing and figures
only as food for our theories. After the boredom of
life and the life of boredom, death, too, adds but little
to our human experiences.

Even more outspoken is the persiflage of Christianity in "Mr. Eliot's Sunday Morning Service," opening with some lines from *The Jew of Malta* ("Look,
look, master, here comes two religious caterpillars").
During the time of service, Sweeney in the bathtub
"shifts from ham to ham." Comical effects are produced by rhymes which belong together only *as
rhymes* and are not connected by an intrinsic logical
meaning, somewhat similar to limericks, although limericks of course have five lines against Eliot's four.
Nonsense-literature later developed in *Old Possum's
Book of Practical Cats* is foreshadowed here.

The last of the poems of the 1920 volume, "Sweeney Among the Nightingales," is introduced by a
Greek motto. The technique, similar to preceding attempts at sarcasm, culminates in the two lines about
the nightingales that "let their liquid siftings fall / To
stain the stiff dishonoured shroud."

This was the end, too, of Eliot's lighthearted, sarcastic, and irresponsible double-talk in poetic form.
The time in which it was written and printed marked
the end of the sentiment of prewar days that all's well
that ends well. The end had not ended well. The

World War hardly made a difference between winners and losers. A historical caesura was made that inaugurated a new and not necessarily better age.

In 1919 Eliot's father had died. In Romantic days, personal experiences of this sort had been a source of literature, but Romanticism was dead, once and for all. There was little leisure and little disposition to write about private sorrows. Literary naturalism, prevalent in Europe for some decades, was on the way out. Eliot, the critic, evolved. *The Sacred Wood,* of 1920, was his first volume of literary reflections. "The contemplation of the horrid or sordid or disgusting, by an artist, is the necessary and negative aspect of the impulse toward the pursuit of beauty,"[20] he said, confirming the ambiguity of his verse.

In this vein Eliot helped express a new universal poetic feeling of the ambiguity of the world. But what was "new" about Eliot's poetry? It was new in the expansion of language, in the use of jargon, slang, banal conversational pieces, foreign words and phrases, literary and scholastic English. Eliot overcame the Puritan canon of literary form, the Victorian paleness and infertility, and enriched the poetry of English-speaking countries by reaching out for new unknown horizons. No doubt, he had the advantage of coming from "outside," a stranger unbound by strict traditions; but his native tongue was English, too. Eliot the American imported fresh perspectives and disturbed the musty atmosphere of poetry that was dominated by Oxford *Books of Verse*. At the same time he was quite aware of the values and potential-

ities of the European-English history to which he went
back despite all revolutionary pathos, especially of the
Elizabethan, metaphysical, and Romantic poets.

American literature for young T. S. Eliot was, as
we heard, useless; English literature of 1920 was of
no great value, either. Yeats, born in 1865, belonged
to the generation before Eliot. James Joyce, six years
older than Eliot, was essentially a prose writer. The
authors of his own generation (D. H. Lawrence, Edith
Sitwell), did not quite make for new literary techniques. Only with and after T. S. Eliot did English
literature receive impulses that were decisive. W. H.
Auden, born in 1907, who emigrated to the United
States, and Stephen Spender, born in 1909, made full
use of Eliot's innovations. The latter's influence also
affected poets in America, especially Archibald Mac-
Leish (for some time self-exiled in Paris), Conrad
Aiken, and Horace Gregory.

Prufrock and Sweeney—they were the new "heroes" of postwar days, somewhat resembling the cari-
catures of a George Grosz. Tristan, Hamlet, Robinson
Crusoe, Don Juan, Kim—these were the heroes of
past ages. Now Babbitt rose, the Philistine, Prufrock
and Sweeney. The "petit bourgeois" became the center, and the title, of poetry. The old aristocrat was
dead, and the proletarian, also a potential figure of
literature, was not to be successfully discovered until
Bert Brecht. Prufrock and Sweeney may have had
proletarian manners, but for a real proletarian they
had too much money, and lacked greatness.

3

The Waste Land

The full success of the new technique, the entire breadth of the new, and at least original, poetic perspective became obvious only with *The Waste Land*. Eliot, still a bank clerk, not always free from financial difficulties, subject to the turbulence of the early twenties, achieved with this poem the rank of one of the foremost European writers. In the same year, 1922, Joyce's *Ulysses* and Rilke's *Duino Elegies* and *Sonnets to Orpheus* were also published.

The Waste Land is a poem in five parts, introduced by Roman numerals, and containing 434 lines (if we do not count the notes). It was, and is, the most important work of Eliot's laboratory, and significantly it is dedicated to Ezra Pound, *"il miglior fabbro."* Pound contributed to the manuscript critically. The main part had been written in the fall of 1921 in Lausanne, where Eliot had, with financial help from Pound, been able to spend some time taking medical treatment; on his return trip he left the manuscript with Pound in Paris. Pound cut it considerably. In October 1922 the poem was published in the journal *The Criterion,* and in November in *The Dial.* Eliot was thirty-four years of age and at the culmination of his literary power, in spite of precarious health and economic instability.

Part I bears the subtitle "The Burial of the Dead," and begins with the famous lines:

> April is the cruellest month, breeding
> Lilacs out of the dead land. . .

The poem wants to convey a mixture of "memory and desire" as the season does which breeds lilacs "out of the dead land." Reminiscences of the *"Starnbergersee,"* of Munich *"Hofgarten,"* of a Lithuanian girl lead us down memory lane. Yet all remains a "heap of broken images" (Heraclitus). These "images," however, are the things that Eliot, the "imagist," clings to. Associations, visions, series of "pictures" follow hard upon each other. Above all hovers the pain of forlornness.

> Son of man,
> You cannot say, or guess, for you know only
> A heap of broken images. . .

Reminiscences, too, of far-away days of Western civilization like quotations from the German text of *Tristan and Isolde* break in with seeming incoherence; but as all civilizations and their various phases are, morphologically speaking, "contemporaneous" (as Ezra Pound holds, or Oswald Spengler in *Decline of the West* and, later, A. J. Toynbee in *A Study of History*), there is justification for such textual combinations and montages. Quotations from Baudelaire, from Webster are strewn in. The scene changes, and we meet Madame Sosostris, "famous clairvoyante," who likewise mixes up the ages, figures, and symbols of civilization in her own irrational manner. This city in which she lives is, indeed, "unreal." In it past, present, and future (at least with Madame Sosostris) are interchangeable. On King William Street ("where Saint Mary Woolnoth kept the hours") one meets a Stetson: Stetson, however, was "with me in the ships at Mylae," *i.e.* at a naval battle that took place about two thousand years ago. In Stetson the ages are unified,

even death and life come to be one and the same
thing, and the subtitle of this part of the poem, refer-
ring to the burial of the dead, can also be turned
around: the dead are reencountered, and the living
meet the dead.

I had not thought death had undone so many.

Stetson, in the end, is recognized as *"mon frère,"* my
brother.

Part II is called "A Game of Chess." Two scenes
make up this part: the chess game, played not out
of interest but out of boredom; and the conversation of
two women about a new set of teeth which one of
them is supposed to get in order to please her husband
who, after four years in the war, is "demobbed." The
first scene, more or less impressionistic, tries again a
review of Western history in a nutshell. History becomes individualized by the itemization of the objects in a room: candelabra, jewels, ivory, perfumes,
candles, pictures, and "other withered stumps of time"
that are "told upon the walls." A woman, lost in this
room, utters the usual words of boredom and loneli-
ness, hysteria and frustration.

> "My nerves are bad to-night. Yes, bad. Stay with me.
> "Speak to me. Why do you never speak. Speak.
> "What are you thinking? What thinking? What?
> "I never know what you are thinking. Think."
>
> I think we are in rat's alley
> Where the dead men lost their bones.

In the other scene, Eliot camouflages his criticism of

society with the talk about the new set of teeth and the husband's return.

> . . . think of poor Albert,
> He's been in the army four years, he wants a
> good time,
> And if you don't give it him, there's others
> will, I said.
> Oh is there, she said.

Jealousy, rivalry between two women. Albert's wife, having had five children already at thirty-one, is trying to get rid of a sixth one with pills.

> The chemist said it would be all right. . .

In both scenes the desolateness of depressive postwar days reigns.

Part III, "The Fire Sermon," leads us to the Thames in early winter. There is no more tourist's trash, and all excursionists have left. Rats are there, and we hear the "rattle of the bones." Words from Spenser, Shakespeare, Verlaine accompany us on our walk along the river bank. The city is "unreal" again. The meaninglessness and infertility of our world is embodied in the blind seer Tiresias, an old man "with wrinkled female breasts" who is described in Eliot's "Notes" at the end of the poem as the "most important personage in the poem, uniting all the rest," although a "mere spectator" (nothing ever *happens* in the poem) and not indeed a "character" at all. "Just as the one-eyed merchant, seller of currants, melts into the Phoenician Sailor, and the latter is not wholly distinct from Ferdinand Prince of Naples, so all the women are one

woman, and the two sexes meet in Tiresias" (note to
line 218). Tiresias is taken from Ovid's *Metamor-
phoses,* Book Three, Verses 320-338. What now does
Eliot's Tiresias, the seer, see? He sees the typist home
at teatime, clearing away breakfast left from the morning, laying out food "in tins," awaiting a young man
who, after the meal she prepared ("she is bored and
tired"), endeavors to "engage her in caresses" which
"still are unreproved, if undesired." The typist is
"assaulted," he encounters "no defense" and "makes a
welcome of indifference." Indifference, boredom, apa-
thy: the waste land of the city, real or unreal. The
typist is glad when her "lover" departs.

"Well now that's done: and I'm glad it's over."

She puts a record on the gramophone. Images rise,
the whining of a mandolin, the river, Elizabeth and
Leicester, Moorgate, Carthage . . . Wagner's *Götter-
dämmerung,* Dante's *Purgatorio,* Augustine's *Confessions,* Buddha's *Fire Sermon* make a bridge from the
world of insignificance to the world of essentials.

Burning burning burning burning

"The complete text of the Buddha's *Fire Sermon,*"
says Eliot in the "Notes," "(which corresponds in importance to the Sermon on the Mount) from which
these words are taken, will be found translated in the
late Henry Clarke Warren's *Buddhism in Translation.*"

O Lord Thou pluckest me out

is a quotation from St. Augustine's *Confessions* again,
and the "collocation of these two representatives of

eastern and western asceticism [i.e. Buddha's and St. Augustine's]," Eliot continues to say in his "Notes," "as the culmination of this part of the poem, is not an accident." *Collocation*—here Eliot uses a term that characterizes very well his new poetic technique of assembling and juxtaposing themes, words, and symbols of various civilizations and ages, "images" which crystallize in an individual poetic mood. However, the fact that he seemed to be in a position in which he had to use the word "burning" four times and, in addition, to say "these words" were *taken* from Buddha, must strike us as either ironic or quite superfluous.

Part IV, by far the shortest (only 10 lines as compared to 76 in the first, 95 in the second, 128 in the third, and 112 in the fifth), carries the subtitle "Death by Water." The only part without notes, it is set in contrast to its preceding part; the fate of Phlebas, who drowned, must be considered a warning not to neglect the aspects of death.

> O you who turn the wheel and look to windward,
> Consider Phlebas, who was once handsome and tall
> as you.

Part V, "What the Thunder Said," leads from the waste land, from fire and water, rocks without water, dead mountains, dead cities, to Indian mysticism. It is the "decay of eastern Europe" that Eliot mainly wants to picture, according to his "Notes." It is, then, a picture of peoples who have lost their God. There are the "falling towers" of Jerusalem, Athens, Alexandria, Vienna, and London, *i.e.* of old Oriental, of ancient West-

ern, and of modern civilization, and thus there is "decay" not only in Eastern, but also in Western Europe.
The Waste Land is generally our land, without water,
without mind, without spirit. "Empty cisterns and
exhausted wells"—tradition seems dead. Eliot repeats
this theme throughout the last part in many variations
("empty chapel," "empty rooms"). "Shantih" is the last
word of the poem, thrice used: it means the "Peace
which passeth understanding," a "formal ending," as
the "Notes" affirm, "to an Upanishad," the Sanskrit
speculative treaties in the late stage of Vedic (ancient
Indian) literature concerned with the nature of man
and the universe.

The general interpretation of *The Waste Land* is
now a matter of course. In the "waste land" of the present day, of our life, which is also a life of flashbacks
into the past and of wishes for the future, there can
only be one path to a meaningful form of human existence that lies beyond the dimensions of time and
space. This path, this *interior* path, this path toward
the inside, must be the concentration of the self upon
the essentials and the dropping of all nonessentials,
however "important" or "interesting" they may seem.
We have to find the eternal in the fleeting phenomena,
the essence in mere existence.

This teaching is, of course, neither new nor revolutionary, and has only draped itself in a new literary
costume. Yet how exciting to observe how modern
literature, unobtrusively, turns to mysticism. This
mysticism goes about incognito. It presents itself anew
to a degree and is so different from Meister Eckhart,

John of the Cross, or Pascal that it may be misunderstood as antimysticism. Contrary to the belief of historians of the Middle Ages or theologians that mysticism could only thrive on the soil of dogmatic-religious,
strictly Christian revelation, the nineteenth and twentieth centuries have proven time and again that mysticism can flower beyond or even against Christianity.
This mysticism, however, will no longer be the report
of a "mystical" experience of the *unio* between man
and God, of vision or ecstasy (and even Meister Eckhart, probably the greatest mystic, never reported such
a *unio*, but dealt in philosophical speculation, belief,
dialectics, in *literature*); it will consist of literary, or
poetic, images. Instead of a *vita*, as in the mysticism
of nuns, or biography, as in Suso, we now have *poetry*.
In this poetry are echoes of "personages" who strive to
overcome the universal split into object and subject.
Eliot gives an example of this mysticism in *The Waste
Land*. His mysticism is an *idea*. The "formal ending" of
the Upanishad, "Shantih," or peace beyond rational
understanding, promises peace either in death or in a
Beyond—or in a mystical realm within the pale of life.

It is strange that critics should point out the individual decay mirrored in present-day literature as if
it were something specifically modern, whereas the
mystics, among others, have always considered the ego,
individuation, the state to be overcome. Certainly the
conditions for these perspectives are different, but the
effect remains the same. The misunderstanding becomes grotesque when, in the wake of T. S. Eliot (or of
de Quincey), people like Aldous Huxley or Henri

Michaux are trying to reach the "*unio mystica*" by way
of mescaline (or something similar). He who lacks
sleep tries the sleeping pill, and he who does not experience the *unio* tries an opiate. Of course, this experi-
ment is not confined to Huxley or Michaux; most conspicuous for comparable attempts, or their description,
are Gottfried Benn's poems "Kokain" and "O Nacht,"
in the tradition of Baudelaire. But neither the state of
intoxication itself nor any "vision" in it caused by drugs
will lead to anything like the true mystical composure.
After intoxication and awakening there remains only
the state of despair, the nonmystical "hangover."

T. S. Eliot, however, fed up with boredom and, as
a Boston skeptic, hardly inclined to play with physical
drugs, turned to religion. In 1948 he said that "any
religion, while it lasts, and on its own level, gives an
apparent meaning to life, provides the frame-work for
a culture, and protects the mass of humanity from boredom and despair."[21] Eliot, a descendant of Puritanism,
sought faith, and he turned to the geographically
closest and ideologically nearest, the Anglican High
Church; not, like so many others of his time (W. H.
Auden, for instance), to something perhaps further
away, to Marxism.

In his *Essays* Eliot has in his own manner confirmed what modern critics say of the decay of the individual—but he said it only of the artist, not of man in
general. "The progress of an artist is a continual self-
sacrifice, a continual extinction of personality."[22] He
has also observed mysticism in literature quite mi-
nutely. In the essay on Dante he speaks of the "mysti-

cal experience"; in that on Pascal he characterizes the antitype of the mystic. Where mysticism begins and where it ends, he knew, and he has never collaborated in the current vague use of the word "mystical." Mystifying interpretations he spurned. He was for a long time on intimate terms with Indian philosophy and, in 1946, expressly pointed out the influence of "Indian thought and sensibility" upon his own opus;[23] he knew quite precisely where he stood as far as mysticism was concerned. But he also warned the scholars interpreting him against reaching too rapid conclusions. He said of Shakespeare that none of his plays had a "meaning," although it would be false to say that they are "meaningless." This is true to an even higher degree of his own *The Waste Land*: the poem's "meaning" is not "mysticism," but the poem is written under certain mystical aspects and emanates thinking related to mysticism.

Deprived of a "story," of a concrete "plot" or "contents," *The Waste Land* nevertheless has by way of the unique conception of the poet an inherent order and "meaning." Poetry is not like philosophy; the demand of critics or readers that poems as well as prose must be "understood" or "understandable" is based upon concepts which stem from logics, and not necessarily from poetry. "Poetry is a constant reminder of all the things that can only be said in one language, and are untranslatable."[24] And this also means that poetry can only be expressed poetically and not logically or scientifically. "The poet makes poetry, the metaphysician makes metaphysics, the bee makes honey, the spider

secretes a filament . . ." The "content" of a poem is
not at all unimportant, however, it is not expressed
logically or chronologically in the poem and not to be
"understood" in such a fashion. The poem must be
looked at as a whole, a totality, which must be poetically recomposed by the reader while reading; philosophy is by the same token not simply "read" but re-
thought philosophically by the reader or student during
his study. Poetry which lives by "images" or "pictures"
must thus be "seen" or "visualized" with the inner eye.
Mysticism is, by definition, the closing of the eyes or
lips and thus seeing blindly or speaking silently,
within: the vision, that is, or the message of a peace
beyond the senses and beyond rationality. *The Waste
Land* constitutes such a "vision" or "message." The
poem leads us thither by the word "Shantih," which we
do not linguistically, rationally, logically, or scientifically "understand"; we must appreciate it, at best,
poetically through the printed image—a word in print
—or through sound, if we do not know what it "means"
and if we have not yet read Eliot's "Notes."

   The Waste Land leads us by necessity into a discussion of the function and the essence of poetry.
Modern poetry, which does not use the old-fashioned
romantic plot, often seems "unclear" because it uses a
novel form of expression that is strange to us. We must
first endeavor to pull it into our orbit of rational understanding, which is no easy task. The modern poem
forms its material, old or new, in a manner that differs
quite radically from poetic techniques of the nineteenth century. The question: "What does the poem

mean?" is meaningless in itself, because poems (old or new), in the first instance, do not "mean" anything, but present something poetically (as modern music or modern painting present something musically or in color and forms that cannot "mean" anything or be "understood" outside of music or color and form).

We must accept poetic images as what they are, *i.e.* images, which are equal in our perception to ideas or sensual experiences; "images" or "ideas" or "experiences" are expressions of other things in reality, which we cannot perceive except through an image or an idea or an experience. All things become known to us through images, ideas, or experiences or the like. Poetic images must be "imagined" or reimagined in our own imagination according to the guiding imagination of the poet, the "imagist."

If today we "understand" and appreciate poems of earlier centuries more easily and readily than those, strangely enough, of our own time, this is mainly so because the older poems have become known and familiar to us in their manner of expression, their values, their choice of words, all communicated through school and society, both lagging behind the avant-garde thought and art. Poems of other ages had to accept the stigma of being called "unclear" by their contemporary critics, as art in general is not always accepted immediately in its age, and often repudiated or even forgotten (like the works of Beethoven in his day, or Bach's in his). Modern poetry, despite its "difficulty" (sometimes with itself), wants, of course, to be accepted and appreciated like all pieces of art; it even

wants to be accepted as a piece of nature. T. S. Eliot
saw the "difficulty" of modern poetry himself, being
part of a "difficult" age growing ever more complex, yet
he insisted on its "nature" ("The poet makes poetry
. . . the bee makes honey").

But, indeed, this poetry did *not* grow as "nature"
does. It does *not* come, as nineteenth-century poetry
mostly did, from emotional values. It does *not* fall from
the tree of creation as a ripe fruit. And most important:
it does *not* come into being without the use of other
older forms of poetry. In other words, the more history
a civilization has, the older it becomes, the more its literature has to sift, digest, use, reuse, repudiate the literature of its former ages. Poetry, too, is culture as a
whole, is history. And it is, above all, a product of
cerebral functions. It is, more so than ever, a product
of a literary consciousness, of construction, of *collocation*, of pieces mounted together.

In this respect modern poetry is in contradiction
to itself, and out of this contradiction further conflicts
arise between author and reader. For what has been
produced by the "brain" consciously, deliberately,
knowingly, like Eliot's poetry, must also be accepted
knowingly. Things which come from the intellect will
be appreciated intellectually and not intuitively.
Things which have been "thought out" can be "thought
over." If a poet, like Eliot, wants to say something that
perhaps is beyond clear and logical expression but
which, at the same time, develops at least "logics of
poetic method" in order to achieve its end, then the
self-contradiction in the resulting poem is obvious and

annoying, too. Eliot's use of quotations represents a scholarly, intellectual, and conscious act. Anything that appears unclear, then, is no longer so by fault of the poem as such, but by fault of the *methods*, of the technique of the poet. Eliot's poetry then no longer just *seems* to be unclear, it is so as a matter of fact, because it wants to weld together heterogeneous elements which stand in each other's way. The fire in such a welding process must be the basic poetic and creative "mood"; and in achieving just such a "mood," Eliot has attained a mastery that lifts him above "poets" who only and mechanically put things together without such "fire" or "mood."

Despite the fact that a great part of Eliot's poems depend upon the use of quotations and consequently provoke rational interpretation, he insists: "*Qua* work of art, the work of art cannot be interpreted; there is nothing to interpret; we can only criticise it according to standards, in comparison to other works of art."[25] Besides, there is a test. "What is surprising about the poetry of Dante is that it is, in one sense, extremely easy to read. It is a test (a positive test, I do not assert that it is always valid negatively) that genuine poetry can communicate before it is understood."[26] This judgment on Dante is important; and what Eliot says about him further can be applied to *The Waste Land*, too.

I do not recommend, in first reading the first canto of the *Inferno*, worrying about the identity of the Leopard, the Lion, or the She-Wolf. It is really better, at the start, not to know or care what they do mean. What we should consider is not so much the meaning of the images, but the reverse process, that which led a man having an idea to express it in images. We have to consider the type of mind which by nature and *practice* tended to express itself in allegory: and for a competent poet, allegory means *clear visual images*. And clear visual images are given much more intensity by having a meaning—we do not need to know what that meaning is, but in our awareness of the image we must be aware that the meaning is there too.[27]

The Waste Land can be read like the *Divina Commedia*: as a walk through Hell and Purgatory to Paradise. Dante, like Eliot, underwent a religious conversion at about the age of thirty-five. The question remains as to whether Eliot is of the same "mental type" as Dante. Does Eliot express himself "naturally" in images or does he do so after long practise? Or: are Eliot's "images" *no* images in the original sense but constructions which underlie certain of his concepts? Is, then, *The Waste Land* as a work of art in no way comparable to the *Divina Commedia*?

The reader must see whether or not in experiencing Eliot's "images" he comes to experience a "meaning." Even if he does it remains open, however, whether or not the reader's meaning is identical with Eliot's. No such absolute identification of the intent of the author and the reception by the reader is, by the way, ever possible. Lecturing in Glasgow in 1942 Eliot himself admitted that the "reader's interpretation may differ from the author's and be equally valid—it may even be better. There may be much more in a poem than the author was aware of."[28] (Or there may be much less in a poem than the author was aware of.)

There are the "frontiers of criticism" of which Eliot spoke in 1956 in Minnesota when he suggested that there "is, in all great poetry, something which must remain unaccountable however complete might be our knowledge of the poet, and that that is what matters most." He condemns the "lemon-squeezer school of criticism" which, "knowing" everything about a poem, still cannot explain what is meant by "creation."[29] Even after mastering vocabulary, spelling, grammar, syntax, social habits, beliefs, learning, and ignorance of the age—*e.g.* of Chaucer—it can still be that one does "not *understand the poetry.*" We have to "enjoy" the "poem as poetry."

The dilemma of such poetry at the same time provoking and rejecting interpretations is best expressed in and through the "Notes" to *The Waste Land* (lacking, by the way, in some editions). These "Notes" are not only problematic in themselves, as we quickly see, but are also paradoxical in the face of Eliot's demand that we "enjoy" poetry as poetry. Such notes are scholarly, but are not poetical or part of poetry. They are not only superfluous, but even disturbing; they do not help us understand poetry, but are in the way of our understanding it as such. They *refute* poetry instead of interpreting it. Eliot's "Notes" are not without parallel (Rilke's *Sonnets to Orpheus* of 1922 have some), but they have set an example—a bad example—more than any other comparable modern literary production.

In addition, these "Notes" are sometimes obscure and do not explain what was to be explained; sometimes they are even quite unintelligible. When Eliot points out that anyone "who is acquainted with these works" (*i.e. The Golden Bough* by Frazer and *From Ritual to Romance* by Jessie L. Weston) "will immediately recognize in the poem certain references to vegetation ceremonies," then he obviously demands that we read those books first, and if we do not, too bad for us. But even those who have read those books, as I have, certainly do *not* "immediately" recognize references to "vegetation ceremonies." And why should they?

Sometimes the "Notes" are simply nonsense, for instance the one to line 199 ("I do not know the origin of the ballad from which these lines are taken; it was reported to be from Sydney, Australia"). That which is quoted from Hermann Hesse (lines 367-377) obviously has been misunderstood by Eliot; his knowledge of German was quite fragmentary. The note to line 221 gives Sappho as source, while the major part of the verse is reminiscent of Robert Louis Stevenson's "Requiem" ("Home is the sailor, home from the sea") and Eliot's continuation "The typist home at teatime" a sarcastic counterpart to Stevenson's "And the hunter home from the hill."

The notes to *The Waste Land* I had at first intended only to put down all the references for my quotations, with a view to spiking the guns of critics of my earlier poems who had accused me of plagiarism. Then, when it came to print *The Waste Land* as a little book—for the poem on its first appearance in *The Dial* and in *The Criterion* had no notes whatever—it was discovered that the poem was inconveniently short, so I set to work to expand the notes, in order to provide a few more pages of printed matter, with the result that they became the remarkable exposition of bogus scholarship that is still on view to-day. I have sometimes thought of getting rid of these notes; but now they can never be unstuck. They have had almost greater popularity than the poem itself—anyone who bought my book of poems, and found that the notes to *The Waste Land* were not in it, would demand his money back. But I don't think that these notes did any harm to other poets: certainly I cannot think of any good contemporary poet who has abused this same practice. . . . No, it is not because of my bad example to other poets that I am penitent: it is because my notes stimulated the wrong kind of interest among the seekers of sources. It was just, no doubt, that I should pay tribute to the work of Miss Jessie Weston; but I regret having sent so many enquirers off on a wild goose chase after Tarot cards and the Holy Grail.[30]

We are back at the beginning. The reader himself must read the poem, intensively, and must let it influence him; and each reader, then, must find his own way to the poem he reads.

With *The Waste Land* Eliot laid the foundation of his later fame. The criticism on *The Waste Land* was divided. Some critics praised it unconditionally; others, like Mégroz, called it the "greatest hoax of the century." In any case, Eliot received the literary award of *The Dial,* two thousand dollars. He seemed on the right path; in *The Criterion,* which he edited, his longest poem had been published and had found, from here, other publishing markets. Eliot had developed something of the instinct of the literary manager. In an age in which editors of literary journals

first think of publishing their own manuscripts Eliot
had made himself publisher. And perhaps here was at
least one publisher who was, at the same time, a poet.

4

~~~~~~~~~~~~~~~~~~~~~~~~~~~~~~~~

Criticism,
Essays,
and
The Hollow
Men

From 1922 until 1939 Eliot was editor of the quarterly review *The Criterion,* in which he published much of his own work that was reprinted later in his *Selected Essays.* During these years—postwar years of tensions, of depression, worldwide economic crises, rise of the European tyrants—up to the outbreak of World War II Eliot developed his politico-cultural ideas. Between the ages of thirty-four and fifty-five he took part actively in literary and in worldly affairs in general. In the fall of 1922, when the first number of *The Criterion,* containing *The Waste Land,* was put out, a new journal and a new poet had entered upon the scene. The result was encouraging. For six months Eliot even undertook to have the journal published monthly, but this attempt failed.

Eliot set as the aim of his journal to bring together "the best in new thinking and new writing in its time" that was available, "from all countries of Europe that had anything to contribute to the common good," as he said in 1946.[31]

[The] review was an ordinary English periodical, but of international scope. I sought, therefore, first to find out who were the best writers, unknown or little known outside of their own country, whose work deserved to be known more widely. Second, I tried to establish relations with those literary periodicals abroad, the aims of which corresponded most nearly to my own. . . . These connections developed very satisfactorily, and it was no fault of any of the editors concerned, if they subsequently languished. . . . And I attribute this failure chiefly to the gradual closing of the mental frontiers of Europe. A kind of cultural autarky followed inevitably upon political and economic autarky. . . . The blight fell first upon our friends in Italy. And after 1933 contributions from Germany became more and more difficult to find. Some of our friends died; some disappeared; some merely became silent. Some went abroad, cut off from their own cultural roots. One of the latest found and the last lost, was that great critic and good European, who died a few months ago: Theodor Haecker. . . . What happened in Spain is more confused; the tumult of the civil war was hardly favourable to thought and creative writing; and that war divided and scattered, even when it did not destroy, many of her ablest writers. In France there was still free intellectual activity, but more and more harassed and limited by political anxieties and forebodings, and by the internal divisions which political propossessions set up. England, though manifesting some symptoms of the same malady, remained apparently intact. But I think that our literature of that period suffered by being more and more restricted to its own resources, as well as by the obsession with politics.

This postscriptum, which Eliot wrote for *The Criterion* in 1946, shows the close contact he had with European literature in the twenties and the thirties. The Bostonian literary apprentice had become in intellect a true European, an *"homme du monde,"* and above all, an *"homme de lettres."* The poet turned critic, the critic worked as literary politician. These seventeen years as editor of a periodical can hardly be considered a diversion, but must be seen as a concentration upon literature. Contrary to representatives of the "lost generation" of Americans in Paris, to Gertrude Stein, Hemingway, MacLeish, Eliot belonged to those who intended to realize certain ethical concepts. (A similar intention of the men of the "lost generation" to realize practically certain political ideas took on form with the beginning of the Spanish Civil War in 1936.)

In those years Eliot's reputation above all as a critic rose. Retrospectively in 1956, Eliot said:

I have been somewhat bewildered to find, from time to time, that I am regarded as one of the ancestors of modern criticism, if too old to be a modern critic myself. Thus in a book which I read recently by an author who is certainly a modern critic, I find a reference to "The New Criticism," by which, he says, "I mean not only the American critics, but the whole critical movement that derives from T. S. Eliot." I don't understand why the author should isolate me so sharply from the American critics; but on the other hand I fail to see any critical movement which can be said to derive from myself, though I hope that as an editor I gave the New Criticism, or some of it, encouragement and an exercise ground in *The Criterion*.[32]

Eliot himself wrote mostly on poets "and poetic dramatists" who had influenced him. Increasingly since 1919 he had published a row of aesthetic-critical essays in different journals. As early as 1920 the first collection of such essays was published, *The Sacred Wood*. Of this group the essay "Tradition and the Individual Talent," of 1919, seems particularly worth mentioning. The European is about to manifest himself; the poet elaborates on his concept of history and time. The

. . . historical sense compels a man to write not merely with his own generation in his bones, but with a feeling that the whole of the literature of Europe from Homer and within it the whole of the literature of his own country has a simultaneous existence and composes a simultaneous order. This historical sense, which is a sense of the timeless as well as of the temporal and of the timeless and of the temporal together, is what makes a writer traditional. And it is at the same time what makes a writer most acutely conscious of his place in time, of his own contemporaneity.[33]

With this "contemporaneity," a concept reminiscent of Spengler's and Toynbee's terminology, Eliot places himself both in the twentieth century and in "world literature." In 1920 he was attracted by Blake and Swinburne. In the following year he showed interest in Dryden and the metaphysical poets. In 1924 he wrote on four other poets of the Elizabethan age. Quite significant is the essay, of 1923, on the "Function of Criticism."

When I say criticism, I mean of course in this place the commentation and exposition of works of art by means of written words. . . . I do not deny that art may be affirmed to serve ends beyond itself; but art is not required to be aware of these ends beyond itself. . . . Criticism, on the other hand, must always profess an end in view. . . . The critic . . . if he is to justify his existence, should endeavour to discipline his personal prejudices and cranks . . . and compose his differences with as many of his fellows as possible, in the common pursuit of true judgment.[34]

Everyday life with its office hours, the worry about the necessary income, the boredom of London banking hours did not devour the poet. Between business hours, tea, lunch, and dinner, after reading of and writing on international commerce and finances, he knew how to liberate himself for his actual task: po-

etry. In this poetry, however, he included his *ennui*
with our business-culture. Three years after *The Waste
Land,* Eliot published another sharp attack upon the
degeneration of his age, in the poem *The Hollow
Men* (1925). The description of boredom of former
days has turned now into the accusation of a mindless
world of figures and facts.

Compared with the previous poem, *The Hollow
Men* is relatively short. It consists of five parts which
again are headed by Roman numerals, about one hundred lines in all.

> We are the hollow men
> We are the stuffed men
> Leaning together
> Headpiece filled with straw . . .

Our voices are "dried," "whisper together," we are
"quiet and meaningless."

> Shape without form, shade without colour,
> Paralysed force, gesture without motion . . .

Those who have "crossed" to "death's other Kingdom"
remember us, if at all, not as "lost souls" but only as
the "hollow men." Even in life we find ourselves in
"the dead land," the dried-out "cactus land." Between
idea and reality is the shadow of our nothingness; we
are hardly in the position to make creation out of conception, existence out of mere potency, love out of
desire.

> *This is the way the world ends*
> *This is the way the world ends*
> *This is the way the world ends*
> *Not with a bang but a whimper.*

Between these verses of accusation and bitterness there is twice, again in italics, the line

For Thine is the Kingdom

pointing to the future. Still, Eliot remains suspended between despair and the possibilities of belief. He has only just opened the door through which he will one day go, both as poet and as man.

In the middle of the twenties, still in search of faith, Eliot revives Sweeney, in "Sweeney Agonistes," an "unfinished poem." He also calls it "Fragments of an Aristophanic Melodrama." It has occasionally been performed on the stage. The meaning of this poem, as Eliot conceives it, is indicated in the motto from St. John of the Cross: "Hence the soul cannot be possessed of the divine union, until it has divested itself of the love of created beings." Sweeney—or Eliot—has not come quite so far.

The first scene of the poem, "Fragment of a Prologue," shows two women, Dusty and Doris, who are being visited by three men, introduced by Sam. The three are an American captain and two American businessmen. Whether British or American, all the persons involved in the scenes reflect the pitifulness of war, postwar, the age, and man. The second scene, "Fragment of an Agon," satirically tells us of the "flight" to a lonely cannibal island (foreshadowing a motif of *The Cocktail Party*). The possibility of Sweeney's serious conversion to a missionary is lost in the farce that Sweeney performs. What in the end remains is this:

Death is life and life is death

One must use "words" when one communicates with
one another.

> I gotta use words when I talk to you
> But if you understand or if you dont
> That's nothing to me and nothing to you
> We all gotta do what we gotta do . . .

The absolute meaninglessness of the circle of day and
night, of being and not-being, is not suspended by the
mere attempt to look beyond the daily circle.

It is London of 1925. T. S. Eliot between house
and office, between office and editing his periodical,
between making money and dialogues with his wife,
between crisis and crisis. If his education in two
American schools and at Harvard, his studies and his
dissertation, his early thoughts and early publications
were not to be in vain, if his expatriation from the
United States and his taking up residence in Europe
were not to be just the exchange of one phase of boredom for the next, if despair was not to be the last
word, then some form of intellectual or spiritual salvation had to follow soon. These were difficult years for
Eliot. And it was not only he who sought new yardsticks, but an entire literary elite which wrote English and was still young. Pound, Hemingway, Stein,
MacLeish, the Sitwells, Lawrence, somewhat later
Auden—they all revolted in their own way. Paris, New
York, Berlin, London: the First World War was slowly
passing over into the Second. The twenty years between 1919 and 1939—what fruitful, what terrible

years—slowly ran out. In St. Louis on the Mississippi time had stood still in those boyhood years before the turn of the century; in Boston the unrest began, New York fell from one stock-market panic into the other, and in London Eliot saw himself in the midst of a world that hardly knew itself any longer between its hope for peace and fear of catastrophe. It seemed to be reserved for the few, for single individuals, to find peace in themselves, if Marxism was not their creed. And it certainly was not T. S. Eliot's.

5

The
Conversion

When in the second half of the "Golden Twenties" Western civilization plunged into the deep universal depression, T. S. Eliot finally knew exactly what he wanted. At this time he experienced his conversion, his turning to acclamation. When others hesitated, he decided for himself. When doors were locked to others, he was offered good positions. He gained a foothold in the literary business world of London; he created for himself a new spiritual, intellectual, commercial, and social home.

In 1926 he joined the publishing house of Faber & Gwyer (later Faber & Faber) and thus came into close contact with contemporary English literature while it was being written. Economically, too, his fortunes rose. With his conversion he had, as Heinrich Heine once put it in regard to himself, the *"entré-billet"* to society. His position put him in one of the centers from which literature was managed and organized. A wide field of activity opened up for him. As one of those who had to help decide what was "good" and "bad" in literature, what was to be rejected and what was to be printed, he could now further his own literary work as well. The poet had climbed into the powerful armchair of the commercial editor. He read what others had written, formed his judgment as to what was "modern" and what "traditional." Poet and critic, editor and poet supplemented each other, under the protecting roof of a publishing house. Eliot's manuscripts reached the hands of the reader and expert, then those of the editor-in-chief, and thence returned to the poet in the form of galley proofs, and finally as a book. A circle was opened up for the poet in which he could live and write.

Not every talent achieves such a relatively fortunate position. Eliot became independent of the favor of strange and possibly hostile publishers competing with one another: and of turns of chance like finding or not finding a congenial editor. He had the opportunity to publish his own works without being dependent on much protection, favor, or plain good luck. However, there was one thing that could endanger Eliot, or any poet: to be without the critical guidance of a man who could read his manuscripts objectively (as Ezra Pound once did). He was always in danger of misjudging himself and publishing things that otherwise, thanks to certain objective literary criteria, would not have been published at all.

In 1926, too, Eliot became Clark lecturer at Trinity College of Cambridge University. A tradition that he had noted in George Santayana, the union of poet and scholar, he now continued in himself. Eliot the intellectual had found a double field of activity, as editor and teacher; the poet in him had to beware of being pushed aside. In the preface to the essay "For Lancelot Andrewes," he formulated his views clearly: he was Anglo-Catholic, Royalist, and literary classicist. In a word, he confessed to being conservative; others called him simply a reactionary. He converted to the Anglican High Church, which has traditionally drawn members of the aristocracy and the academic. Eliot, the descendant of Puritans who had left England to gain religious freedom, had returned into the lap of the old Church, whether more liberal and tolerant or not. The American republican became a monarchist, the literary revolutionary of *The Waste Land* became the poet of conversion or reversion. But one is free to consider this act of Eliot's instead as a revolution, in the conservative sense, or even as a reaction, a new evaluation of the old. In any case, Eliot moved progressively backward. He was now an *écrivain engagé*, whatever this might be, surely not on the social-radical or Marxist-Communist side, as was prevalent in the twenties, but on the ultraconservative side.

But sometimes the extremes touch each other. We know that Ezra Pound, too, represented a literature that was "engaged," whether on the side of restorationist politics or of anarchy is perhaps hard to say; he went to Fascist Italy which was ruled syndicalistically by the ex-Marxist Mussolini. W. H. Auden, whom Eliot influenced aesthetically, went from rather social-minded England to the supposedly liberal America, where he was prosecuted as a "Communist fellow traveler." Pound and Auden, at least, erred in their respective choice of new home countries. Whether Eliot found what he was looking for, or whether he only adjusted to prevailing circumstances, is something that only he could have answered for himself. We find little that can justify a biographer's doubt about Eliot's satisfaction with the choice he had made. To be sure, he continued to see certain negative aspects of our industrial evolution and of our material "progress," and he cannot be regarded as blind to social questions. The step back which Eliot, in a

way, made with his conversion is not so rare with enlightened minds or liberals as one might think. Eliot
no longer was the cool Bostonian skeptic accepting
neither tradition nor progress; he had once been close
to absolute despair, and now he entered into the spiritual realm of absolute faith. He himself, at least, regarded his development as logical. Polemics against
his conversion did not touch him much. To a man who
in 1930 saw only "progressive degradation," as he said
in the essay on Baudelaire—and for whom there was
no such thing as progress in religion or art—any criticism of his attitude must have been utterly unimportant. In 1929 he took the last step back; he became a
naturalized British subject.

From this time on we can follow the controversy
over whether Eliot is an "American" or an "English"
author. (This question is not quite as futile as that as
to whether Rilke, for instance, was a "German" or an
"Austrian" poet; for Germany and Austria had for a
very long time something like a common literary history.) Eliot considered himself an "English" poet; he
stood in the English literary tradition and continued it
with his work. As far as American literature is concerned, only Poe meant something to him, and he considered Poe a European, intellectually. Literary critics sometimes have counted Eliot among English,
sometimes among American authors. In 1950, Louis
Untermeyer dealt with Eliot in *Modern American Poetry* and omitted him from *Modern British Poetry*,
which was published the same year. E. Legouis and
L. Cazamian accept him as English in their *A History*

of English Literature (1954), and when in 1956 Van
Wyck Brooks and Otto L. Bettmann published *Our
Literary Heritage,* a history of American literature,
they did not include Eliot.

The decisive factors in such decisions tend to be
the author's own choice and his intellectual and artistic position, rather than his place of birth, passport,
denomination; and in both intellectual and artistic
respects, T. S. Eliot belongs to the Old World. Joseph
Conrad was, by birth, a Pole, and today his work is
among the classics of English literature. T. S. Eliot
came from St. Louis, left the United States for good
when he was twenty-six years old, published his important works in England, and found his place beside
"metaphysical poets." Geography and nationality, race
and religion cease to have meaning when intellectual,
artistic, ideological, and literary classifications are to
be made. In Eliot's case, furthermore, it is important
that he was, from the beginning of his school life and
career, disposed toward England, the home of his ancestors. In *Four Quartets* he uses the name of the village from which his forefather had migrated to America—"East Coker" is here more than a name, it is the
location of his deepest roots.

Quite typical for the European community of
English provenience that Eliot now represented more
or less officially, are the comments he made in 1929
about Dante, which later came to be an homage for
Shakespeare as well. Dante, for Eliot, was the perfec-
tion of literary language. Whereas Shakespeare por-
trayed a wider range of the spectrum of human life,

Dante saw deeper into the abyss and at the same time strove higher for spiritual values. Both Dante and Shakespeare were masters of their craft, up to whose level of attainment no third writer ever reached. "Shakespeare understands a greater extent and variety of human life than Dante; but . . . Dante understands deeper degrees of degradation and higher degrees of exaltation."[35]

This acknowledgment of European literary values, following immediately upon conversion and naturalization, this grateful respect toward the most Catholic of all poets—Dante—and the most acclaimed of all British dramatists—Shakespeare—shows how solidly he wished to anchor in both religion and patriotism. Consequently his success and his fame spread among those who, like Eliot, believed in those two poles of traditional society. Still, the *Encyclopaedia Britannica* of 1929 does not mention him, seven years after the publication of *The Waste Land.* Eliot remained what he did not want to remain, esoteric.

A visible sign of Eliot's conversion was the poem *Ash Wednesday,* issued in 1930 by Faber & Faber, the publisher who employed him. (In that year also his mother died; the most genuine tie to his home country had been cut.) Some verses of the poem had already been printed in 1927 (later to become the second part of the poem), in 1928 (the first part), and in 1929 (the third part). The entire poem consists of six parts with more than two hundred lines; it is introduced by a dedication to his wife (which is lacking in the complete edition of 1950). Ash Wednesday: the day on

which Catholics remind themselves that all is mortal,
transitory, and vain. Ash Wednesday is also the beginning of fasting and abstinence. In the beginning the
mood that is presented by Eliot—now about forty years
of age—is hopelessness. Age and weakness have
reached him. Knowledge of the fundamental ignorance
of man takes hold of him. However, another source of
knowledge is discovered.

> Because I know that time is always time
> And place is always and only place
> And what is actual is actual only for one time
> And only for one place
> I rejoice that things are as they are . . .

The simple turn toward reality seems made. But behind the simple reality, as we know it, lies the second
and real reality as we do *not* know it, of the trans-
cendental.

> Consequently I rejoice, having to construct some-
> thing
> Upon which to rejoice . . .

The thing that he turns to is, actually, faith.

> And pray to God to have mercy upon us
> And I pray . . .

Not enough, man who discusses his matters "with himself" rests his faith too much upon the objective and
absolute essence of God himself.

> Pray for us sinners now and at the hour of our death
> Pray for us now and at the hour of our death.

Bones become dust. But in the mystical union that
the "white Lady" promises, in the second part of the

poem, rests salvation. Eliot utilizes certain motifs from the mysticism of John of the Cross. The "speech-lessness" of man is countered by the word of God. The "*sanctum silentium,*" the "*oratio silentii*" is indicated by Eliot in such phrases as "Speech without word and / Word of no speech." The "waste land" of the early Eliot becomes now the "land" where "neither division nor unity" matters.

This is the land. We have our inheritance. This is Eliot's land of faith and love. The "ascent" of the third part leads from despair to hope and thence to death and eternity. Eliot speaks of "stairs" which he ascends, three in all. Beyond the third stair, "beyond hope and despair," he finds his aim, though negatively, because:

Lord, I am not worthy . . .

The fourth part is characterized by the vision of the dry rock which finally "springs up," the vision of the liberation from time and from dream. The fifth part is the praise of the "Word without a word, the Word within / The world and for the world," God's word. But this Word is not heard here because "there is not enough silence." In the sixth and last part the initial motif of hopelessness is reused ("Although I do not hope"), but it is transcended by the calling of the "Blessèd sister, holy mother, spirit of the fountain," the prayer for peace and the unification with the Divine.

Suffer me not to be separated

And let my cry come unto Thee.

He who demands of mysticism that it must promise, announce, or even report of that mystical union with the Divine thinks perhaps too much of the *vitae* of medieval nuns in which the last union with the Divine is spoken of ecstatically or visionarily. But this women's mysticism is not free from certain pathological features and is by no means the climax of mystical literature. In the writings of Meister Eckhart, Tauler, Seuse, St. John of the Cross, only the possibility of the *unio mystica* is spoken of. The most beautiful fruit of the literature—or philosophy—of mysticism is, above all, sublime speculation, courageous confession, composed edification, a high literary form. The famous mystics we know of were *writers*. They were masters of their own language and often, like Eckhart, founders of new literary idioms. Eliot stands in the tradition of such literary or poetic mysticism of the "negative" sort which strives toward liberation from earthly things, from the ego and the will, but which does not know attainment of its goal in life. Eliot speaks of this dilemma in the second part:

> End of the endless
> Journey to no end
> Conclusion of all that
> Is inconclusible
> Speech without word and
> Word of no speech
> Grace to the Mother
> For the Garden
> Where all love ends.

T. S. Eliot, city bred, an urbane type, enlightened by twentieth-century science, had found his way back to where priests, monks, shoemaker-prophets, and "Romantics" had been before him. The sharp, cold intellect, missing, often enough, its object, approaches irrationality again. Where logics failed, the paradox won out. It is worth while to remember the path of this new "mystic" Eliot: he came from learning and philosophy to poetry, history, and criticism; he had been bank clerk, editor, publisher, businessman; he stood in the very hub of universal literary life, not Boston, but London. One should, perhaps, remember the habits of this modern intellectual. A cultivated man, the elegance of the London City, the gentleman with Derby hat and umbrella. And now one should look, again, at *Ash Wednesday*. Then one starts wondering whether the man behind the tailored suit is one to whom the soul is more important than business or whether he is one who wears a false mask. Perhaps, in London, the best mask is that which does not strike one as such. Those who doubt Eliot's sincerity may call his "mysticism" a literary flirt with esotericism, an extravaganza in the monotony, in the boredom, in the *ennui*, in the "waste land" of our civilization, a fashion like Yoga or astrology, a play with Kabbala in the age of interviews with the moon, and publicity around the golden calf of Progress. But he must also think of the fact that just as one who offers a little finger to the devil stands in danger of being taken by his whole hand, a man like T. S. Eliot must have reckoned with the possibility that the tempter of angels may be carried away by them.

Eliot's conversion was followed by the first collection of his writing. There were also the first conspicuous honors. In 1925 the *Poems 1909-1925* had been published by Faber & Faber; now, in 1932, the *Selected Essays* came out. These essays dealt with literature, aesthetics, theology, philosophy. In the enlarged edition of 1936 Eliot dwells on what literary criticism should be: it should start from a definite ethical and theological point of view. Though he still holds that only literary yardsticks can determine what literature is, he goes on to say that the greatness of literature cannot be measured solely by literary concepts. The critic who, so far, had only been a critic was now augmented by the Christian, the member of the Anglican High Church.

In 1932 Eliot returned, for the first time since his voluntary expatriation, to the United States. Almost twenty years had elapsed since he left Harvard and turned away from an academic career. He did not return as a lost son, but as a celebrated writer. His guest professorship at Harvard was almost a national event that went beyond the borders of Cambridge, Boston, New England, and the East Coast. He gave "reticent teas" at which expectant young intelligentsia would watch "the silent poet eat cake." Eliot tended to fall asleep in club armchairs but believed that his brain worked as well as ever after he had his cup of tea.

Harvard did not give him any honorary degrees, but Columbia University conferred upon him the title of Litt. D., *Literarum Doctor*. The man with a dissertation but without the degree now received his doctor's cap.

Eliot's fortune did not remain unclouded; in 1933 he was divorced. Forty-five years old, an accomplished writer, he continued his literary way unmoved. This way led within. *The Rock,* a play, from which ten "choruses" were printed in 1934, is Eliot's manifesto after his conversion. In ten scenes on almost twenty pages we find both accusation and sermon. In the change of seasons, "of spring and autumn, birth and dying," we gain knowledge "of motion, but not of stillness," knowledge of speech, "but not of silence," knowledge of words and "ignorance of the Word."

> All our knowledge brings us nearer to our ignorance,
> All our ignorance brings us nearer to death,
> But nearness to death no nearer to God.
> Where is the Life we have lost in living?
> Where is the wisdom we have lost in knowledge?
> Where is the knowledge we have lost in information?
> The cycles of Heaven in twenty centuries
> Bring us farther from GOD and nearer to the Dust.

This form of accusation is well known to the reader of Western literature, from the history of religion and theology, from the lives of philosophers and saints. Since Eliot specifically refers to "ignorance," one is tempted to draw parallels at least to Nicholas of Cusa, philosopher and mystic, who from a negative attitude toward the world came to see the *"coincidentia oppositorum,"* the unification of opposites in God; man's wisdom is to recognize his ignorance (*de docta ignorantia*).

According to Eliot, neither death nor twenty centuries of Christianity have brought us closer to God, only closer to dust. The man of the city wants "chop-houses," instead of churches, he wants physical instead of spiritual food. The "Rock" appears (Peter was called by Jesus "Kephas," Rock). His message:

Make perfect your will.

It is not the harvest that counts, but the sowing. We must perpetually struggle between Good and Evil.

> The desert is squeezed in the tube-train next to you,
> The desert is in the heart of your brother.

The "waste land" is, still, our presence. The "workmen" are chanting:

> In the vacant places
> We will build with new bricks
> There are hands and machines
> And clay for new brick
> And lime for new mortar
> Where the bricks are fallen
> We will build with new stone
> Where the beams are rotten
> We will build with new timbers
> Where the word is unspoken
> We will build with new speech
> There is work together
> A Church for all
> And a job for each
> Every man to his work.

The answer comes from the "Unemployed."

> No man has hired us
> With pocketed hands
> And lowered faces

> We stand about in open places
> And shiver in unlit rooms.
> Only the wind moves
> Over empty fields, untilled
> Where the plough rests, at an angle
> To the furrow. In this land
> There shall be one cigarette to two men,
> To two women one half pint of bitter
> Ale. In this land
> No man has hired us.
> Our life is unwelcome, our death
> Unmentioned in "The Times."

Eliot presents here a Christendom that finally becomes aware of its social mission. Yet the perspectives
remain imperfect. Also, it is not the "right" relationship between man and man that counts, but the right
relationship between man and God. On the other
hand, however, the relationship between man and God
should be an example for that between man and man.

In the second scene the "values" of worldly man
are condemned: imperial expansion, industrial development, merely intellectual enlightenment, prints of
the Bible, superficial things.

> The British race assured of a mission
> Performed it, but left much at home unsure.

Eliot, British by choice, is now in a position to criticize
certain specifically English wants, and he criticizes
them as well from supernational, *i.e.*, Christian points
of view. During a time of prosperity, people will
neglect "the Temple," and "in time of adversity / they
will decry it." The Church, for Eliot, must always be

built anew; for the Church is "the Body of Christ in-
carnate." Our civilization is on the wrong road. Many,
he says self-accusingly in the third scene, "are engaged in writing books and printing them" because
they desire to "see their names in print"; much is being
read, but the word of God is not. What is it then that
remains after all our errors? The obituary above our
ruins:

> And the wind shall say: "Here were decent godless
> people:
> Their only monument the asphalt road
> And a thousand lost golf balls."

The perfect refrigerator, the working out of rational
morality, the printing of as many books as possible:
that is our "culture," our "humanity."

> Life you may evade, but Death you shall not.

Time and again Eliot, the writer, calls for "silence" in
the Babelic confusion of our language; time and again
he laments the writing of books. This is Eliot's paradoxical situation: the writer condemns writing. The
writer can write polemically, but he has not the power,
like the man who stops writing or whatever it is that
he does, to become a saint. He writes of the saint,
without taking upon himself the self-denial of the
saint. Eliot remains *"littérateur"*—yet even in such an
attitude he is not so different from the mystics, or
"mystics," who wrote, from Eckhart to Yeats.

In the next parts of the poem Eliot analyzes human history, "systems," "higher religions," "reason":

> And then Money, and Power, and what they call Life,
> or Race, or Dialectic.
>
> . . . .
>
> In an age which advances progressively backwards?

Eliot rejects all the things which are sacred to newspapers and thus to mankind. The only thing that remains is, again, faith. Only faith can save us.

1915 to 1925: that was the T. S. Eliot of Prufrock and Sweeney, the poet of disillusionment, the critical intellectual, the skeptic, the searcher. Until the age of almost forty Eliot held back. 1925 to 1935: that was the Eliot of the conversion and of naturalization, the poet of religious verse, the faithful. At the end of his forties his life's path has become straight. The step from *The Waste Land* to the poem of *The Rock* was definitive. The choice of words for the titles —*waste land* to *rock*—is symbolical enough.

'During these years A. J. Toynbee as well became convinced that salvation for Western civilization could not come from our "cultural heritage," our vulgar materialism without Marx, but from within, from religion *against* Marx; contrary to Spengler who, as is apparent from his *Decline of the West*, did not believe in such spiritual values and who, in his book *Prussianism and Socialism*, foresaw another, a doubtful political solution which, indeed, turned out to be catastrophe (Hitler's fight against Marx). Farther east in Europe, Socialism with Marx and without Prussianism was tried out and survived other forms of regeneration. Eliot did not stand alone with his demands in the

City of London of his time; in England religious reformerdom had always been kept alive down into certain spheres of the working classes and into the Labour
Party. Eliot, naturally, placed reformerdom on the
political right wing. As a poet he considered his pen
the proper tool for proclaiming his aims. The stage
then seemed to him the best medium for reaching
greater segments of the people. Consequently he
turned to playwriting in the next years.

One year after *The Rock* he gathered his poems
and published them, in 1936, as *Collected Poems
1909-1935*. Little that was truly great was to follow.

6

*Festival-Plays,
Drama,
Nonsense*

There are numerous references in Eliot's essays and criticisms which refer to plays and the theater in general. The "Dialogue on Dramatic Poetry" (1928) analyzes the possibilities of the "poetic drama" in our time. Drama as "the perfect and ideal drama" is to be found "in the ceremony of the Mass."[36] In 1919, Eliot had dealt with " 'Rhetoric' and Poetic Drama." Euripides (1920) and Seneca (1927) occupied him, as did the playwrights of the Elizabethan age. He was at home with Marlowe, Shakespeare, and Ben Jonson just as much as with modern playwrights like Shaw, O'Neill, Pirandello, and Ernst Toller, or with modern stage practicians like Max Reinhardt, Gordon Craig, Meyerhold in the Soviet Union, and Gustav Gründgens in Germany. His bent for "conversation," dialogues, and everyday language in poetry seems to have been a talent for the spoken word of the stage as well; his emphasis on "direct speech" (*Essays*) or on "ordinary" language throughout his work points to his conviction that only "the changing language of common intercourse" can convey anything.[37]

Among the great poets of world literature there are but few who have tried their luck successfully at playwriting; and among the great playwrights of world literature we have but few great poets. Shakespeare, despite his sonnets, and Rilke are masters in one field only. Goethe may, perhaps, be the exception. That Eliot the poet tended toward dialogue from the beginning, and Eliot the playwright did not stop writing poetry, may speak against or for him; in any case, his double activity or talent was both characteristic and dangerous for him. *Murder in the Cathedral* (1935) was Eliot's first full-grown dramatic poem or poetical drama. Would modern idiomatic expression and time-honored tradition here be united? Would the material yield to modern forms of expression? These questions were directed toward modern play-writing as a whole. Shakespeare, the great model, was not to be remodeled. Ibsen, the liberator of modern theater, had already been put aside. Dramatic expression was a more or less Continental affair. What could naturalism and slang, what could the aestheticizing reading-dramas of Neo-Romanticism contribute to contemporary theater? Retrospectively Eliot said, in 1953:

Twenty years ago I was commissioned to write a pageant play to be called *The Rock*. The invitation to write the words for this spectacle . . . came at a moment when I seemed to myself to have exhausted my meagre poetic gifts, and to have nothing more to say. . . . The task was clearly laid out: I had only to write the words of prose dialogue for scenes of the usual historical pageant pattern, for which I had been given a scenario. I had also to provide a number of choral passages in verse. . . . This chorus of *The Rock* was not a dramatic voice; though many lines were distributed, the personages were unindividuated. . . . The chorus in *Murder in the Cathedral* does, I think, represent some advance in dramatic development: that is to say, I set myself the task of writing lines, not for an anonymous chorus, but for a chorus of women of Canterbury—one might almost say, charwomen of Canterbury.[38]

Eliot succeeded in combining "sacred" contents with prosaic and yet poetical texts. It was a type of play that combined the "ceremony of the Mass" with modern stage technique and poetry. With *Murder in the Cathedral* Eliot made, as he himself found, certain progress in the shaping of the chorus; the persons of the chorus became more individual, and the chorus as a whole has now become a specific body, the "Women of Canterbury." Reviewers acknowledge that the theater had a new, even inspiring form of the religiously motivated play.

When I wrote *Murder in the Cathedral* I had the advantage for a beginner, of an occasion which called for a subject generally admitted to be suitable for verse. . . . Furthermore, my play was to be produced for a rather special kind of audience—an audience of those serious people who go to "festivals" and expect to have to put up with poetry. . . . And finally it was a religious play. . . . I wanted to bring home to the audience the contemporary relevance of the situation. The style therefore had to be *neutral*, committed neither to the present nor to the past. As for the versification, I was only aware at this stage that the essential was to avoid any echo of Shakespeare. . . . An avoidance of too much iambic, some use of alliteration, and occasional unexpected rhyme, helped to distinguish the versification from that of the nineteenth century.[39]

Murder in the Cathedral was first published as a stage edition for the "Festival of the Friends of Canterbury Cathedral," then as a book by Faber & Faber. New editions followed in rapid succession. Later the play was made into a movie with T. S. Eliot participating in the production. Ildebrando Pizetti wrote the music for an opera, using the play as libretto.

The hero of the play is the martyred Archbishop

Thomas Becket. Eliot created a dramatic frame which
consists of the chorus of the women of Canterbury,
three priests, and followers of the King. Especially in
the parts of the chorus do we observe Eliot, the poet.
The two parts of the play are held together—or kept
apart—by an "Interlude": the Archbishop is preaching
on Christmas Morning of the year 1170. After Becket's
murder the four knights advance to the front of the
stage and address the audience directly, thus destroying the illusions of the audience and breaking with the
conservative style of plays. The specific problem, the
actual "conflict," begins on the last five pages of
the printed version.

This finishing dialogue is written with great subtlety and intelligence. The First Knight appeals to the
audience's belief in "fair play" ("You are Englishmen") and is, at the same time, aware of the fact that
the murder ("one man being set upon by four") was
not honorable. "Nevertheless"—he appeals to the audience's "sense of honor": "You are Englishmen, and
therefore will not judge anybody without hearing both
sides of the case." The Second Knight declares that in
what they have done they "have been perfectly disin-
terested." They are not "getting anything out of this."
The entirely perfidious argument of the knightly class
is brought out very effectively by Eliot. We see the
brutal knight ("I had drunk a good deal") who, after
sobering up, denies all responsibility and makes an
excuse of his "duty." The Third Knight turns the whole
case around; Becket himself is guilty: he committed
treason by "openly" abandoning "every policy that he

had heretofore supported" as Chancellor and affirm-
ing, as Archbishop, that there was a higher order than
that which the King, and he as the King's servant, had
for so many years striven to establish. "We have been
instrumental in bringing about the state of affairs that
you approve. We have served your interests; we merit
your applause; and if there is any guilt whatever in
the matter, you must share it with us." The Fourth
Knight puts an apparently paradoxical question:
"Who killed the Archbishop?" Not the knights! No,
Thomas Becket not only provoked the murder—in fact,
he committed "Suicide while of Unsound Mind."

Thus, in the name of "fair play," "honor," "reason,"
and "justice" the truth is completely twisted around
with arguments that are cunning and sophisticated to
such a degree that they "convince" the audience of the
contrary of what they have seen before. Here Eliot not
only brands, as he has often done, certain defects of
his own age, not an isolated case, but the mentality of
certain social agents of British history for the purpose
of generally condemning human behavior in parallel
conflicts. The basic evils of man, violence, ambition,
vanity, cowardice, insincerity, perfidy, brutality, mean-
ness are subjected to scrutiny. These all-too-human
weaknesses are confronted with the strength of a man
like Thomas Becket, the saint, the rock of the Church
amidst a kingdom in turmoil.

The step from the ivory tower of the poet down
to the stage of the world was taken rather late by
Eliot. And the consequences were rather mild. One
year after the festival play, in 1936, Eliot the critic

reappeared. *Essays Ancient and Modern* was published. Public honors followed. In 1937 the University of Edinburgh conferred upon him an honorary doctor's degree; one year later the University of Cambridge followed suit. As a gift in return for the society which held him in such high esteem he published in 1939 his essay "The Idea of a Christian Society." It was the year of the outbreak of the Second World War, the deepest cut into European, Western history and civilization for centuries. Of "Christianity" not much was left in that year, in the years leading up to the outbreak of hostilities, or in those following it.

In the same year two other volumes by Eliot appeared: *The Family Reunion* and *Old Possum's Book of Practical Cats*—two volumes that had almost nothing in common except the name of the author and the publishing company of Faber & Faber.

The Family Reunion had its London premiere in March 1939, in Westminster Theatre. The play, no longer historically oriented like *Murder in the Cathedral*, dealt with people of our time. Versification was, as Eliot said in his Harvard lecture, the first problem. He developed a line that despite its variable length still had one caesura and three stresses. With his chorus and his dramatis personae he had, it seems, great difficulties; they remained quite artificial. The entire play contains too many descriptions of detail and situation and too little action. The exposition is drawn out. The plot (taken from Aeschylus) was disappointing. Twelve years after the premiere Eliot himself considered the play as a whole a failure. The conflict, similarly to that of *Murder in the Cathedral,* revolves around guilt and expiation (atonement); a murder is to be repented. The family meets on the occasion of Amy's birthday. Harry, Amy's son, tries his hand as a missionary. Like Becket, he chooses the narrow path of the saint. He attempts to cure himself inwardly. Mythology is turned into the psychology of religion and faith. The play reminds us in its motivation somewhat of Albert Schweitzer's mission in Africa, but seems to lack essential convincing artistic quality.

After this play *Old Possum's Book of Practical Cats* came out. Three things seem to be important for the genesis of the cat book, in the writing of which Eliot was "assisted," as he said in its dedication, by the encouragement, criticism, and suggestions of friends: the love for cats of the English, the English sense of dry intellectual nonsense, and Eliot's own general fun with and talent for rhymes. The beginning at once refers to another famous volume, *Alice's Adventures in Wonderland,* by hinting at the "mad hatter." Of course, the success of this book had to be limited to the English-speaking world outside of which it could not, not even in the best translation, be fully appreciated; and no translation of that unique book has even been satisfactory.

So this is this, and that is that:
And there's how you AD-DRESS A CAT.

7

Four Quartets

The trip to Dublin, in 1940, for a lecture on Yeats interrupted Eliot's residence in London at the time when the "Battle for Britain" was fought. In 1942, when the war was in the balance, he spoke about "The Music of Poetry" in the University of Glasgow. After the festival play, drama, the book on cats, and criticism, poetry again began to hold Eliot's major interest when the fate of the West was quite open. The "endless adventure" of poetic writing, and of life, continued.

Although numerous obligations to society must have distracted Eliot considerably, he always seemed to know where the limit must be drawn. He was an ardent letter writer, contributed toward welfare undertakings like the Red Cross, wrote introductions, prefaces, and essays, spoke over the radio, edited anthologies of Kipling and Joyce, took part in church conferences, held speeches—what had come from Eliot's pen in the way of poetry during those hard years was a question well worth asking.

In 1943 Eliot, fifty-five years old, published his *Four Quartets*, which had been in the making from 1940 to 1943. The first edition of that poem came out in New York, and in 1944 the British edition followed. Both editions together were issued in about ten thousand copies. The *Four Quartets* belongs to the most mature of Eliot's works. If it is correct to say, as Eliot did, that modern poetry must "learn" from past poetry; if his method of choosing, of citing, of mounting other poetry, if then *eclecticism* was correct," i.e. "modern"; if a modern poet must thus have a wide range of knowledge and critical judgment and be master in the use of construction (things that Eliot had practised from *The Waste Land* to *Ash Wednesday*)—then today only the mature poet of advanced years can give his best. Only the poet who overlooks the history of poetry will enrich this history with something new. The *Four Quartets* have been placed on the rank of the *Duino Elegies* by Rilke, Hölderlin's late hymns, and Dante's *Divina Commedia*. Addition and synthesis, formerly abrupt in Eliot's practise, have become milder and more harmonious, and a soft lyrical tone melts the four parts of the poem into one homogeneous whole.

The hint of the title toward music, toward Beethoven's late work, had been prepared by Eliot for a long time. Early in his career he made use of musical concepts. In the essay "The Music of Poetry," 1942, he speaks in the language of the composer about the essence of poetry: about dissonance, cacophony, rhythm; verse shows a relation to the development of a theme by various instruments: "there are possibilities of transition in a poem comparable to the different movements of a symphony or a quartet; there are possibilities of contrapuntal arrangement of subject-matter."[40] Soon the critics discovered the structural relationship of the *Four Quartets* to Beethoven's last quartets (op. 127, 130 to 132, 135). As early as 1935 Stephen Spender had already submitted the suggestion that *Ash Wednesday* showed a relation to Beethoven's quartet composition.

Four Quartets makes reference to the four elements, the four ages of man, the four seasons; three-

dimensional space is completed by time, the fourth
dimension, and time's three dimensions are completed
by the fourth, eternity. "Burnt Norton," the first part,
is a country home which Eliot inhabited in Glouces-
tershire. Two questions from Heraclitus (cited in the
original, from the German edition of Diels's *Die Frag-
mente der Vorsokratiker*) immediately place the
reader before difficult language problems. The poem
itself begins with references to the various dimensions
of time.

> Time present and time past
> Are both perhaps present in time future,
> And time future contained in time past.
> If all time is eternally present
> All time is unredeemable.
> What might have been is an abstraction
> Remaining a perpetual possibility
> Only in a world of speculation.
> What might have been and what has been
> Point to one end, which is always present.

Upon the *leitmotif* of these complex philosophical in-
dications we have the variations. As far as "reality" is
concerned: "human kind" cannot "bear very much
reality." But contrary to the unrest of the world there
is the "still point" of the eternal center around which
everything, including time, revolves: God. What God
is, cannot be said, for then God would not be God.
God rests outside of time. Man must gain inner freedom to approach God.

> The release from action and suffering, release from
>   the inner
> And the outer compulsion . . .

is exactly that behavior or form of existence which the old mystics had preached centuries ago. (The German concept of *"Gelassenheit"* which, by way of Heidegger's *"Eingelassenheit"* came to be Sartre's "engagement," a political variation of reactivation in the world, means just that "release" which Eliot preaches.) Eliot significantly quotes the German term *"Erhebung"*:

Erhebung without motion—

—not so much, perhaps, because there is no equivalent in English (lifting, rising, raising, exaltation, elevation, transcending; also collecting or revolting or revolutionizing indicate what the German word contains) but in order to characterize the special, "strange" situation of eternal rest. He uses a "foreign" word in order to picture the "foreign," unknown, the difficult or even impossible. In any case, we cannot stay in such a situation, being "lifted" without motion, for long; time pulls man back into the world of the flesh. The "temporaneity" of human existence, as Heidegger said, is man's most congenial fate. Time versus no time, man against God are the eternal confrontations—motion against stillness, words against silence.

"East Coker," the second part, is that village from which the Eliots migrated to the new world.

In my beginning is my end.

The circle closes. Houses rise and fall and rise again. The motif of the first line, beginning and end, is repeated. Old and New England become moments of eternity. Eliot interrupts himself and says:

> That was a way of putting it—not very satisfactory
> A periphrastic study in a worn-out poetical fashion,
> Leaving one still with the intolerable wrestle
> With words and meanings. The poetry does not
>   matter.

The critic, apparently, overcomes the aging poet. Dissatisfaction with words, with the written thing, with something like pure literature and literature only, is expressed rather spontaneously. The poet breaks through his own poetry, he finds himself at an end.

> There is, it seems to us,
> At best, only a limited value
> In the knowledge derived from experience.

As in *The Rock*, writing is disqualified by the writer. This is something different from "Romantic irony" or "Weltschmerz": it seems the breakdown of form and human creation. What remains is, again, a "belonging to another, or to others, or to God."

> The only wisdom we can hope to acquire
> Is the wisdom of humility: humility is endless.

The houses are all gone. The dancers are all dead. Death remains for man, and darkness. Everything is doomed and everybody, captains, bankers, men of letters, patrons of art, statesmen, civil servants, industrial lords, the Stock Exchange. . . .

> And we all go with them, into the silent funeral,
> Nobody's funeral, for there is no one to bury.

What is the "meaning" of our life? Ignorance, dispossession, humility.

And what you do not know is the only thing you know
And what you own is what you do not own
And where you are is where you are not.

In other words, self-denial, poverty, death, and eternity are the aims of the mystic, of the saint. The ego
arrives at itself only when it gives itself up and reaches
the nonego, God. Our health is, in reality, disease; in
fact, our "only health is the disease."

The whole earth is our hospital.

Blood and flesh must go. *Hoc est corpus meum.* Good
Friday of Christianity. The beginning motif is now
turned around:

In my end is my beginning.

The explanation of the title of the third part, "The Dry
Salvages," is given in the text itself. "The Dry Salvages
. . . is a small group of rocks, with a beacon, off the
N.E. coast of Cape Ann, Massachusetts." Eliot knew
the place from the vacations of his youth. With the
image of "the river" Eliot goes even further back into
his youth, to the Mississippi. The river's rhythm was
"present in the nursery bedroom," in the "rank ailan-
thus of the April dooryard," in the "smell of grapes
on the autumn table" and "the evening circle in the
winter gaslight." This is, again, St. Louis of before
1900.

The river that is within us is complemented by
the sea that is all about us. River and sea are the to-
kens of reality on which our memory rests. Worldly
success here and the meaning of life there—two sides

of existence—stand opposite each other without com-
plementing each other harmoniously. History and the
aims of life are not connected with each other, they
stray apart. What is our aim? Again, as at the end of
The Waste Land, Indian philosophy is referred to.

> I sometimes wonder if that is what Krishna meant—
> Among other things—or one way of putting the same
>   thing:
> That the future is a faded song . . .
> And the way up is the way down, the way forward is
>   the way back.

After Eliot practised the skepticism of *The Waste
Land*, however, he had converted to the Anglican High
Church. Krishna is supported by the "lady," "Queen
of Heaven" whose prayer alone brings salvation from
the endless cycle of life. Science and "progress" are
nothing; only the "point of intersection of the timeless / With time" is an "occupation for the saint":
"Selflessness and self-surrender," old mystical terms
for the overcoming of the ego and the reaching of
something absolute beyond the relativity of time and
life. Whether these terms and ideas go back to John
of the Cross or to Angelus Silesius, whether to Spanish, French, or German mysticism—in any case, ba-
roque feelings of *vanitas vanitatis*, of medieval desire
for deliverance become manifest.] Eliot's occupation
with the literature of the seventeenth century, especially with John Donne, break through again.[Man
must become that which he strives for in the end.

> You are the music
> While the music lasts.

There are only hints, Eliot says, as to what man can or must do. Man is something to be overcome. He searches for a twofold identity: for himself psychologically and for an identity with something objective existentially. The subject—man—must become an object in true and absolute being. Such striving for "identity" found expression elsewhere at about the same time, for instance in Rilke's verses, the *Sonnets to Orpheus*—"if drinking is bitter to you, become wine" (second part XXIX). The rest, Eliot holds, is "prayer, observance, discipline, thought and action."

> The hint half guessed, the gift half understood, is Incarnation.
> Here the impossible union
> Of spheres of existence is actual . . .

The mystical union, although impossible, appears as the highest goal. For most people it is, indeed, unattainable. The trying is everything. The saint may in the end reach the goal.

"Little Gidding," the fourth part, leads us back to an Anglican religious community in Huntingdonshire of the seventeenth century. "Midwinter spring" characterizes again the "impossible" union of opposites, the *"coincidentia oppositorum,"* "pentecostal fire" in the "dark time of the year." Here in Little Gidding, as in every other place of the world, is the "world's end"; but here, too, in this special place, "Now and in England," one kneels down to pray. Eliot now clearly says what he is driving at. The lines that follow in verse can be considered prose as well. "There are three conditions," he says, "which often look alike / Yet differ completely, flourish in the same hedgerow: / Attachment to self and to things and to persons, detachment / From self and from things and from persons; and, growing between them, indifference / Which resembles the others as death resembles life." At the cost of poetry perhaps, Eliot prefers to state his case logically. He draws the sum of his life. Once he attached himself, as in his love of a country; now he detaches himself in an absolute way, in an essential way, he becomes "renewed, transfigured, in another pattern." His essential task Eliot puts now in quotations from the English mystic Julian of Norwich of the fourteenth century, a contemporary of another important female mystic, Mechthild of Magdeburg. It is quite significant to read Eliot here in context. At the end of *Four Quartets* he says two things: 1) The end is only a beginning, and 2) only in the right use of words can we communicate such a message. The mystic meets with the writer, the writer as a writer must here necessarily surpass the mystic as long as he *is*.

> What we call the beginning is often the end
> And to make an end is to make a beginning.
> The end is where we start from. And every phrase
> And sentence that is right (where every word is at
>   home,
> Taking its place to support the others,
> The word neither diffident nor ostentatious,
> An easy commerce of the old and the new,
> The common word exact within vulgarity,
> The formal word precise but not pedantic,
> The complete consort dancing together)

> Every phrase and every sentence is an end and
>   beginning,
> Every poem an epitaph. And any action
> Is a step to the block, to the fire, down the sea's throat
> Or to an illegible stone: and that is where we start.
> We die with the dying:
> See, they depart, and we go with them.
> We are born with the dead . . .

The poem finishes with the paradoxical promise:

> And the fire and the rose are one.

This is the face of modern mysticism. Mysticism is for the reader of the twentieth century, for the reader of Eliot, Rilke, Yeats, Mallarmé, something that is strange and unfamiliar, something of past centuries. Yet it seems always present, in literature, in poetry, even in some forms of existentialism. Sooner or later the poet, dissatisfied with the arch between the poles of subject and object, finds his way to the union of the poles. He breaks down the tension between the opposites. Mysticism here means paradoxical writing and the giving up of rational ideas about truth. It means an opening for the *whole* world as the poet sees it. Instead of with vision or ecstasy, instead of with hallucination or stigmatization, modern *literary* mysticism begins with criticism of the surroundings and of the self, with dissatisfaction with civilization; this is followed by inversion or conversion and by an opening toward such spheres of being as heretofore were excluded from reflection. In the face of the importance of modern mysticism for poetry one is tempted to say that to a certain degree such mysticism is a criterion of quality.

The teaching of the philosopher Bradley, on whom Eliot wrote his dissertation, was that the "ultimate fact is experience which means indissoluble unity with the perceived." This theory prepared certain convictions of the older Eliot, the man of mysticism. If Meinong says that an object is something that stands opposite us, toward which our mind can direct itself, a correlation to all intentional acts, to all things that can be "meant" or "intended," as *e.g.* even a square circle (which, outside "intention," does not exist), then Eliot had already learned in his early student days that there are things which are real though paradoxical. The "square circle," for example, is replaced in *Four Quartets* by the "intended" union of opposites or two things that otherwise exclude each other, by absolutely different things such as man and God. The "square circle" finds its nonmathematical but mystical solution in the *unio mystica.* The intellectual and rationalist, the Anglo-Saxon empiricist made a one hundred-and-eighty-degree turn and became an irrationalist, a "mystic," standing closer to Bergson than to Bertrand Russell, closer to Pascal and John of the Cross and Plato than to Descartes or Aristotle, closer to Europe than to John Dewey's new pragmatic America. Eliot renewed mysticism in the spirit of Puritanism, he announced the coming of the mystic in the City of London.

8

Honors

The war was over, and the days and nights as well in which Eliot had been active in the air-raid warning system. As early as 1945 Eliot visited Paris and lectured on "The Social Function of Poetry," something he had talked on before in London in 1943. Eliot remains somewhat vague about the social function of poetry, does not include specifically its political function and believes in a social use "for the whole of the people of the poet's language, whether they are aware of his existence or not."[41] In his radio talk on "The Unity of European Culture," published in German in 1946, he emphasized after the catastrophe of World War II all those intellectual and spiritual values which seemed to have been lost. Nothing of hate or revenge. Eliot was peaceful, almost cordial, and he proved that at least *he* was quite serious in his Christianity.

In 1948 he received the Nobel Prize for Literature. At the age of sixty he got the highest recognition which the literary world could confer upon any living author. After Kipling (1907), the Indian Tagore (1913), Yeats (1923), Shaw (1925), and Galsworthy (1932) he was the sixth British subject to be honored in this way. Now Eliot's fame reached those circles which up to then had not been initiated into his esoteric writings; the Penguin Book *Selected Poems*, with the major part of the poems of the edition of 1936, was put out in an edition of fifty thousand copies.

In 1947 Harvard finally conferred upon Eliot an honorary doctor's degree. Princeton and Yale followed suit. One year later in Great Britain he received one of the highest medals of the Empire, the Order of Merit. Oxford added yet another doctor's cap.

In 1950 Eliot published *The Cocktail Party.* The title itself promised universal success. The premières in London and New York carried Eliot's name throughout the world. Continental stages performed the play. Yet there was not much that was new in Eliot's philosophy; what his poetry had proclaimed for a very long time, for a generation, was now popularized in dramatic dialogues. The poetic messages of former days become somewhat clearer in dramatic form, but also more superficial and diluted. One year after the première Eliot lectured on the play at Harvard. He holds ("Poetry and Drama," 1951) that in *The Cocktail Party* he endeavored to avoid "some of the errors" of *The Family Reunion.*

To begin with, no chorus, and no ghosts. I was still inclined to go to a Greek dramatist for my theme, but I was determined to do so merely as a point of departure, and to conceal the origins so well that nobody would identify them until I pointed them out myself. In this at least I have been successful; for no one of my acquaintance (and no dramatic critics) recognized the source of my story in the *Alcestis* of Euripides. . . . In the second place, I laid down for myself the ascetic rule to avoid poetry which could not stand the test of strict dramatic utility. . . . And finally, I tried to keep in mind that in a play, from time to time, something should happen; that the audience should be kept in the constant expectation that something is going to happen; and that, when it does happen, it should be different, but not too different, from what the audience had been led to expect.[42]

The play is called "A Comedy." Apart from the marriage conflict of the Chamberlaynes, the play re-

volves around the fate of Celia Coplestone. In the
emptiness and the stupidity, in the business methods
and the meaninglessness of the modern world, there
is a young woman who is ready to seek her own ego,
to sacrifice it, to overcome herself and to give others
an example through her martyrdom. After social conflicts, Celia joins a religious order which obliges her to
active Christian help. In Kinkanja among the natives
there is the plague, followed by an insurrection, and
Celia is crucified by the natives. What "meaning," if
any, does this sacrifice have? Sir Henry Harcourt-
Reilly, the strange guest, half psychoanalyst, half
priest, offers the explanation: Celia was doomed.

> When I first met Miss Coplestone, in this room,
> I saw the image, standing behind her chair,
> Of a Celia Coplestone whose face showed the aston-
> ishment
> Of the first five minutes after a violent death.

It was obvious, he continues, that "here was a woman
under sentence of death. / That was her destiny." But
she herself had to choose the "way of life" which "led
to death," her own death. Eliot here seems to have
used part of the ontology of Heidegger which, through
Sartre, had been a public good of those years, the
"being toward death." Man who, although "thrown into
life," chooses his own death is the only individually
living man. There is generally in this play much of
existentialism, which after 1945 was in vogue in Europe. Eliot, in any case, tried to be as modern as he
could. Toward the end of the first act Edward says:

> There was a door
> And I could not open it. I could not touch the handle.
> Why could I not walk out of my prison?
> What is hell? Hell is oneself,
> Hell is alone, the other figures in it
> Merely projections—

These words seem a mixture out of Freud, Kafka, and Sartre, only slightly banal. Existentialism, psychoanalysis, surrealism, and Christianity in the sense of Albert Schweitzer are cast upon a Broadway stage in the attractive wrappings of a cocktail party. The "saints" who are cited by Reilly in the middle of the second act are similar to Celia and to the hero from Albert Camus' *The Plague*. The problem of making decisions as the center of philosophical discussion dominated in those years after the war. "Engagement," with Sartre, was the motto, and Eliot taught "engagement," "decision," "participation," too, only in contrast to Sartre and the atheist-Marxist existential schools of thought and in line with Christian principles. Eliot lectured on *Christian* engagement, somewhat obscured by flimsy conversations at cocktail parties. Peter Quilpe is Celia's counterpart, he is "engaged" by Hollywood and makes movies, while his former friend Celia dies the death of a Christian martyr.

Human isolation, so Eliot says in *The Cocktail Party*, can be overcome by active participation in the salvation of the world. Solitude must be overcome by individual choice of action. At the bottom of that choice faith must lie.

The kind of faith that issues from despair. Reilly

says to Celia before she embarks on her journey to
Africa and death:

> Go in peace, my daughter.
> Work out your salvation with diligence.

But in all humanness, we suspect, there is some inhu-
manness in letting a young girl go on to her death like
that instead of trying to work out a salvation that is
rational, social, and free of traces of psychopathology.
Where the border lies between humanism and bar-
barism in Reilly's message (which in itself wavers between psychoanalysis and fraud) no one seems exactly to know. It is somewhat cheap to satisfy the
modern reader with a sort of witchcraft and astrology
("I saw the image, standing behind her chair") that
Celia, the Christian, wants to destroy: not in London,
but in Africa. And if it is not hocus-pocus and super-
stition that Eliot practises here, then it must be considered the sheer irony of a comedy in Wilde's or
Shaw's manner.

Eliot's style of dialogue is, in addition, a somewhat elevated Wilde *and* Shaw, partly witty, partly
shocking, partly commonplace. The marriage drama
of the Chamberlaynes approaches Strindberg without
Strindberg's demoniac quality. Social criticism does
not reach Brecht's dimensions: it has little knowledge
of the social roots of the evil. The play may even di-
vert from real social problems for the sake of religion.
Everything that is absurd with Ionesco becomes at
best paradoxical with Eliot. Eliot seems to have used

the stage for a sort of dramatic construction that should perhaps be only read. His comedy presents itself as a compromise between a moral message and a popular play. All that is really controversial is eased up, real passions are diluted. Celia may perhaps be the exception; but as Eliot himself admits, that part of the comedy that reflects Celia's fate is but "epilogue" and not dramatically inherent. Celia's fate is not demonstrated on the stage. It is only talked about. Her fate is far away. At a cocktail party a glimpse of real life is caught. Those times are gone when beasts and saints, Richard and Jeanne d'Arc, Becket and his murderers came upon the stage in person. Any trace of dramatic and Shakespearean radicalism and realism is conspicuously absent. Eliot keeps his distance from the plot that he wants to deal with. Thus Sir Reilly's message, which he only presents and does not subject himself to, must leave us cold, a message that faith must result from despair. Who has despaired? It remains a message from the writer, who remains backstage. Eliot the poet considers himself at best a medium, a mirror of his own life and not a mirror of life as a whole.

At Harvard there was, however, the common conviction that Eliot, even before *The Cocktail Party*, was the greatest living Anglo-Saxon poet, although perhaps not as famous as Sandburg or Frost, and that *The Cocktail Party* would further enhance his fame. The man who expressed such convictions was Archibald MacLeish, who in the twenties had also been a European exile, who had been influenced by Eliot, and who now, in 1950, was a Harvard professor of rhetoric and oratory. He called Eliot a representative of the "dislocation" of the American artist.[43] Eliot, in truth, would rather have chosen to live in the slums of London, as he confessed himself, than in the United States; for there was something that he feared more than slums, the endless row of houses on a street like a band, over which rolls an unending stream of cars.[44] And there was something that he judged much more valuable than certain geographical aspects; intellectual aspects.

Forty-five years earlier Eliot had enrolled at Harvard. Now new students of a new generation sat in front of him when he lectured about "Poetry and Drama" in his old alma mater. *The Waste Land* had in the meantime become literary history and the theme of graduate courses as an example of modern literature of almost a generation. In 1951 Eliot gave account of himself. He saw himself as a writer who had not accidentally returned time and again to writing plays. He introduced himself as a playwright. But his own conviction of his ability as a dramatist did not further his experiments with the stage. *The Confidential Clerk*, published in 1954 by Faber & Faber, did not change the general view that Eliot was rather a poet than a writer of effective dialogues. The play was inspired by *Ion* of Euripides. Euripides, too, handled mythological material freely and projected it into customs and problems of his own time. Eliot in turn changed Attica into England. The problem, on the surface, is that of the identification of a child by his parents. The real problem deals with certain questions of guilt, with the search for an authentic form of life. Simpkins, the clerk, exemplifies this search. He too goes inward; he too (as is prophesied) will take over a spiritual mission.

Eliot, the "dislocated" artist, overcame more and more the European continent which had once lured him. In 1954 he was awarded the Hanseatic Goethe prize of the City of Hamburg. His address at Hamburg University, in May of the following year, dealt with "Goethe as the Sage." It is part of the inner biography of Eliot that he had approached Goethe only very slowly and hesitatingly, almost at odds with him. It took him a lifetime to do justice to the author of *Faust*. This may have been partly due to the geographical distance that separated Eliot from Germany; partly due to the fact that Anglo-Saxons, unlike the French, hardly ever had a ready access to German literature (with such exceptions as Bulwer-Lytton or Carlyle in England and Emerson in America); partly due to Eliot's preference of Dante and Shakespeare, whose greatness stood between him and Goethe; partly due to simple misunderstandings. Hints upon Goethe as a critic (*Essays*) or as poet are untroubled by any knowledge in the matter; to call Baudelaire a "late and limited Goethe" and to place Wordsworth next to Goethe[45] is simply nonsense. It probably had nothing to do with literary criticism that Eliot in 1933, the year Hitler came to power, called Goethe a man who "dabbled in both philosophy and poetry and made no great success of either."[46] In 1944, in the

Presidential Address to the Virgil Society, published
in 1945, he said that Goethe's poetry, because of its
"partiality, of the impermanence of some of its contents, and the germanism of the sensibility," appears
to the foreign eye "limited by his age, by his language,
and by his culture, so that he is unrepresentative of
the whole European tradition, and, like our own nineteenth-century authors, a little provincial," and "we
cannot call him a *universal* classic."[47] In 1954, though,
after being awarded the Goethe prize he confessed:
"For anyone like myself, who combines a Catholic
cast of mind, a Calvinistic heritage, and a Puritanical
temperament, Goethe does indeed present some ob-
stacles to be surmounted."[48] In Hamburg Goethe is,
finally, "one of the Great Europeans," together with
Dante and Shakespeare. But even in Hamburg Eliot
evades his true task, to deal with Goethe the writer;
almost half of the lecture deals with something else.

In 1956 Eliot revisited the United States. Almost
seventy years of age, he remembered, while lecture-
touring in Minnesota, the hours of learning with Ezra
Pound (who, at that time, was in an asylum in Washington, D.C., condemned for treason having escaped
the penitentiary only because of his mental health).
Retrospects upon his youth and early success, personal
fortune and misfortune accompany Eliot in these
months. In 1957, ten years after the death of his first
wife, he remarried (and dedicated to his second wife
his book *On Poetry and Poets*).

From Munich he received in 1958 the honor of
becoming corresponding member of the Bavarian

Academy of Fine Arts. Lake Starnberg, Hofgarten, Munich acquaintances with the German girl from Lithuania who forbids him to consider her a Russian: these were things of before 1914 which had been set down in *The Waste Land* of 1922. The "heap of broken images" proved its durability. The University of Rome conferred upon him another doctor's degree, Florence awarded him a gold medal for extraordinary achievements as translator of Dante.

In 1959 Eliot published *The Elder Statesman.* The play, going back again to themes of Greek drama, the *Oedipus of Colonus* by Sophocles, draws life's sum. Did Eliot feel like his Lord Claverton, the elder statesman, who has not the slightest desire for the life which he left behind and only fear of the vacuum that is before him? Eliot still has the power to work which Claverton is lacking. Claverton is sick unto death. He waits for nothing, or for "Nothing." Was Eliot just as disillusioned as Claverton after farewell banquets, honors, and speeches? Claverton does not know what affected him more, the insincerity of the speeches on him or that of his replies. His daughter consoles him with the fact that he was at the zenith of his fame when he withdrew from active life. Claverton knows better; what he read in the newspapers was the usual thing in journalism, and in ten years his death would only evoke a short note. His son-in-law also consoles him: such ingratitude must be the fate of every man in public life. Claverton, however, sees himself as one of the "successful failures."

At the time that this play was being written,

some critics had already questioned Eliot's success as a writer. One of the most profound studies, Grover Smith's *T. S. Eliot's Poetry and Plays,* finished with the evaluation that even at best Eliot's strange, private vision is directed inwardly toward an isolated self; and that he, despite the greatness of some of his poetry, never learned to bring the passions of all sorts of people into his art.[49]

Eliot had to confront himself in those years with his own criticism and that of others; Lord Claverton reflects upon this situation without being necessarily an autobiographical figure. Claverton looks back; Gomez-Culverwell, the old friend, appears and sharpens his vision for the past. Claverton as a student ran over an old man with his car and escaped; now he tries to get rid of this guilt. He flees from himself. Gomez represents his bad conscience. Claverton's escape into a sanatorium does not help because the sanatorium is but a duplication of the civilization which produced it, it is more fiction than reality—instead of sincere silence there is the quiet room with television. Old reminiscences and acquaintances appear, like Mrs. Carghill, his former mistress. Claverton had once acted shabbily toward her.

Another bad failure is Claverton's son, Michael. He represents the "prolongation" of his father. Something that he, the father, never admits is self-understood as far as his son is concerned, guilt. His son functions as but another means of denying his own guilt. The first recollection of Michael is that he was blamed for something that he had not done; but if someone always gets blamed it is clear that he eventually will run into trouble. The argument seems halfway brilliant, but is deceptive. Even Michael only uses psychological arguments in order to deny his guilt. He wants to get away from it all, overseas perhaps, he wants to be himself. But Claverton says that this would be flight. And he who flees always loses the race. One cannot get rid of the ghosts of one's past and enter the new, late reality. Claverton's confession of his former flight is the first step into a new meaningful life; his confession that he allowed himself to be "bought away" from the marriage with Maisie—Mrs. Carghill—is the second step. Liberation seems near. Claverton now has the real inner peace which is a result of penitence; and penitence is a result of seeing the truth. And beyond and above truth is love.

The contents of the play indicates once again the message of Eliot's former poetry. Boredom and *ennui* now seem overcome. But even faith has its weak moments. As early as 1930 in the essay on Baudelaire Eliot spoke of the possibility of damnation: "and the possibility of damnation is so immense a relief in a world of electoral reform, plebiscites, sex reform and dress reform, that damnation itself is an immediate form of salvation—of salvation from the *ennui* of modern life, because it at last gives some significance to living."[50] If Lord Claverton in old age must still struggle for faith one may think of Eliot who, in *The Elder Statesman,* expressed what he might have felt himself: that in the end not faith in itself is what matters and what remains, but the *dialectics* of faith and defection, of engagement and boredom, of salvation and condemnation, a living and growing faith that is always on the verge of being lost and therefore always present in a never tiring consciousness.

9

A Life's
Sum

With the year 1960 T. S. Eliot had received the degree of *doctor honoris causa* twenty-three times. The young man with a dissertation but without a corresponding title seemed fully rehabilitated. Perhaps the honors from Harvard and Princeton, from the first years after the war, were meaningful; but what was the fifteenth or twentieth doctor's cap to indicate to a man who according to his own poetry thought nothing of such celebrations whatsoever?

> Of dowager Mrs. Phlaccus, and Professor and Mrs.
> Cheetah
> I remember a slice of lemon, and a bitten macaroon—

He said in the poem "Mr. Apollinax," and in the first act of *The Elder Statesman:*

> I don't know which impressed me more, the
> insincerity
> Of what was said about me, or of my reply · · ·

Or had the scholar, the critic, the editor, the businessman and publisher forgotten what the poet once said in "The Rock"?

> And they write innumerable books; being too vain
> and distracted
> for silence.

There were voices that expressed the belief Eliot the critic had been more important than Eliot the poet. No doubt, his play on images remained esoteric; his diction is, often academically, codified; he expresses himself obscurely; and what is supposed to be a symbol turns out to be a scholastic formula. Like a ven-

118

triloquist Eliot works with puppets; we see various faces, yet despite all variations we hear only *one voice*. Eliot's significance lies in his literary technique of collecting, applying, reshaping and rewording known phrases and ideas in something like a poetic melting pot. In this respect he follows Ezra Pound, *"il miglior fabbro."* His citations, associations, reminiscences may, in the last analysis, be considered a poetic "anthology" of verse. What makes Eliot modern is his technique; what was once expression through him became cutting and mounting. But his poetry knows how to cover up that technique and to create atmosphere and color. The reader may have in various ways become suspicious of Eliot's lines, but he allows himself to be led by the stream and the music of Eliot's words. He may not always understand what he reads—and possibly enjoys—but he will wait till the end with certain pressing questions.

Eliot himself was skeptical of his talent. Once in every five or ten years, he confessed, there is "inspiration"; the rest is practise and patience.[51] All his life Eliot was plagued by two doubts: Would the poetry that he wrote have lasting value? Would the next piece of work be as "good" as the last? Eliot, to be sure, found the breakthrough to himself.

Death is life, and life is death . . .

But whether there was, however, a breakthrough of the poet toward the reader remains doubtful and will have to be decided by literary history in the next decades. For a time we were familiar with a naturalized

Englishman, member of clubs like the Athenaeum, the "Arrow Collar man" who drinks his tea, his sherry, his Burgundy, the administrator of a successful publishing house with his office on dignified Russell Square in the heart of London, in Bloomsbury where he worked for over thirty years and whence came punctually the friendly, cool letters. Russell Square had made literary history even before Eliot when it played a role in Thackeray's *Vanity Fair*—a motif which may stand above the entire work of T. S. Eliot.

He died on January 5, 1965, and was buried in East Coker, that little village of Somerset county whence in the seventeenth century his forefathers had migrated to a land that turned out not to be God's own country at all. East Coker (*Four Quartets*):

In my beginning is my end.

Eliot was cremated. The urn is kept in St. Michael's Church of the village.

In my end is my beginning.

We do not know whether what Eliot said is right. Yet we know from *Four Quartets:*

We have existed
Which is not to be found in our obituaries · · ·

Notes

1. Introduction

1. "The Frontiers of Criticism," *On Poetry and Poets* (New York: The Noonday Press, 1961), p. 123.
2. *ibid.*, p. 127.
3. "Shakespeare and the Stoicism of Seneca," *Selected Essays* (New York: Harcourt Brace and Company, 1950), p. 118.
4. "Goethe as the Sage," *On Poetry and Poets*, pp. 259-60.
5. "Baudelaire," *Selected Essays,* p. 373.
6. "Four Quartets," *The Complete Poems and Plays* (New York: Harcourt, Brace & World, Inc., 1962), p. 130.
7. "Goethe as the Sage," p. 243.
8. "Yeats," *On Poetry and Poets*, pp. 295-6.
9. *ibid.*, p. 306.
10. "The Unity of European Culture," *Notes Towards the Definition of Culture* (London: Faber & Faber, 1962), p. 112.
11. "Goethe as the Sage," p. 245.

2.   Prufrock

12.   *The Literary Essays of Ezra Pound*, ed. by T. S. Eliot (Norfolk, Conn.: New Directions, 1954), pp. 3ff.
13.   "The Three Voices of Poetry," *On Poetry and Poets*, pp. 103-4.
14.   "The Unity of European Culture," pp. 110-11.
15.   *ibid.*, pp. 111-12.
16.   "Yeats," p. 296.
17.   Jacket photograph by Kay Bell.
18.   H. Lüdeke, *Geschichte der amerikanischen Literatur* (Bern, 1952), p. 544.
19.   "Baudelaire," *Selected Essays*, p. 375.
20.   *The Sacred Wood* (London, 1920), p. 153.

3.   The Waste Land

21.   *Notes Towards the Definition of Culture*, p. 34.
22.   *Selected Essays*, p. 7.
23.   *Notes Towards the Definition of Culture*, p. 113.
24.   *On Poetry and Poets*, pp. 13-14.
25.   *Selected Essays*, p. 122.
26.   *ibid.*, p. 200.
27.   *ibid.*, p. 204.
28.   *On Poetry and Poets*, p. 23.
29.   *ibid.*, pp. 124-5.
30.   *ibid.*, pp. 121-2.

4.   *Criticism, Essays and* The Hollow Men

31.   *Notes Towards the Definition of Culture*, pp. 115ff.
32.   *On Poetry and Poets*, p. 117.

33. *Selected Essays*, p. 4.
34. *ibid.*, pp. 13-14.

5. *The Conversion*

35. *Selected Essays*, p. 214.

6. *Festival-Plays, Drama, Nonsense*

36. *ibid.*, p. 35.
37. *On Poetry and Poets*, p. 21.
38. *ibid.*, pp. 98f.
39. *ibid.*, pp. 84f.

7. Four Quartets

40. *ibid.*, p. 32.

8. *Honors*

41. *ibid.*, p. 15.
42. *Selected Essays*, pp. 91-2.
43. "Der Künstler in der Gesellschaft," *Das Literarische Deutschland* (May 20, 1951).
44. K. Smidt, *Poetry and Belief in the Work of T. S. Eliot* (London, 1961), p. 24.
45. *Notes Towards the Definition of Culture*, p. 112.
46. *On Poetry and Poets*, p. 256.
47. *ibid.*, pp. 69-70.
48. *ibid.*, p. 243.

49. G. Smith, Jr., *T. S. Eliot's Poetry and Plays* (Chicago, 1958, 2nd ed.).
50. *Selected Essays*, pp. 378f.

9. *A Life's Sum*

51. K. Smidt, *op. cit.*, p. 31.

Bibliography

Major publications by T. S. Eliot

Prufrock and Other Observations (poetry), 1917
Ezra Pound: His Metric and Poetry (criticism), 1917
Tradition and Individual Talent (criticism), 1917
Poems (poetry), 1920
The Sacred Wood (essays), 1920
The Waste Land (poetry), 1922
*Homage to Dryden: Three Essays on Poetry of the Seven-
 teenth Century* (criticism), 1924
The Hollow Men (poetry), 1925
Journey of the Magi (poetry), 1927
For Lancelot Andrewes: Essays on Style and Order (criti-
 cism), 1928
Ash Wednesday (poetry), 1930
Anabasis (translation of poem by Saint-John Perse), 1930
The Use of Poetry and the Use of Criticism (criticism),
 1933
After Strange Gods (essays), 1934
The Rock (drama), 1934
Elizabethan Essays (criticism), 1934
Murder in the Cathedral (drama), 1935
Essays Ancient and Modern (essays), 1936
Collected Poems 1909-1935 (poetry), 1936
The Family Reunion (drama), 1939
Old Possum's Book of Practical Cats (poetry), 1939

The Idea of a Christian Society (essays), 1939
Four Quartets (poetry), 1943
What Is a Classic? (essays), 1945
Notes Towards the Definition of a Culture (essays), 1948
The Cocktail Party (drama), 1950
Selected Essays (essays), 1951
Complete Poems and Plays 1909-1950, 1952
The Three Voices of Poetry (essays), 1954
The Confidential Clerk (drama), 1954
Essays on Elizabethan Drama (criticism), 1956
On Poetry and Poets (criticism), 1957
The Elder Statesman (drama), 1959
Selected Poems (poetry), 1961
Collected Plays (drama), 1962
Knowledge and Experience in the Philosophy of F. H. Bradley (doctoral dissertation, 1916), 1964
To Criticize the Critic (essays), 1965

Works about T. S. Eliot

Browne, E. M., *The Making of T. S. Eliot's Plays,* 1969
Freed, Lewis, *T. S. Eliot: Aesthetics and History,* 1962
Gallup, D., *Bibliographical Checklist of the Writings of T. S. Eliot,* 1947
Gardner, Helen, *The Art of T. S. Eliot,* 1950
Kenner, Hugh, *The Invisible Poet: T. S. Eliot,* 1959
Mathiessen, F. O., *The Achievement of T. S. Eliot,* 1935
Rajan, B., ed., *T. S. Eliot: A Study of His Writings by Several Hands,* 1948
Smith, Carol M., *T. S. Eliot's Dramatic Theory and Practice,* 1963
Tambimuttu, M. J., ed., *T. S. Eliot: A Symposium,* 1948
Tate, Allen, ed., *T. S. Eliot: The Man and His Work,* 1966
Williamson, George, *A Reader's Guide to T. S. Eliot,* 1955
Williamson, H. H., *The Poetry of T. S. Eliot,* 1932
Ungar, Leonard, *T. S. Eliot: Moments and Patterns,* 1966

Index

Harvard University, 7, 8,
    22, 23, 76, 105, 109,
    110, 118
Hawthorne, Nathaniel, 4
Heidegger, Martin, 11, 95,
    106
Heine, Heinrich, 30, 66
Hemingway, Ernest, 14, 29,
    57, 62
Heraclitus, 37, 94
Hesse, Hermann, 52
High Wycombe Grammar
    School, 23
"Hippopotamus, The," 31,
    32
*History of English Litera-
    ture, A* (Legouis
    and Cazamian),
    69–70
Hölderlin, Johann, 93
Hollow Men, The, 60–61
Huckleberry Finn (Twain),
    4
"Humoresque," 8
Husserl, Edmund
    influence on Eliot, 9, 11
Huxley, Aldous, 43, 46
"Hysteria," 26

Ibsen, Henrik, 88
"Idea of a Christian So-
    ciety," 89
imagism, 16–17, 37, 41
Ion (Euripides), 110
irony, 31
    romantic, 30, 96

James, Henry, 22, 24
James, William
    influence on Eliot, 9, 11

Jew of Malta, The (Mar-
    lowe), 32
John of the Cross, 43, 61,
    73, 74, 98, 102
Jonson, Ben, 84
Joyce, James, 12, 34, 36
Julian of Norwich, 100

Kafka, Franz, 107
    wish toward transforma-
        tion, 21
Kipling, Rudyard, 104
"Kokain" (Benn), 44
"Krebsbaracke" (Benn), 18

Laforgue, Jules
    influence on Eliot, 8
Lawrence, D. H., 34, 62
    imagism, 17
Legouis, E., 69–70
Lewis, Sinclair, 6
life-philosophy, 12
Lloyd's Bank, 23
*Lloyd's Bank Economic
    Review,* 23
Lotze, Rudolf Hermann, 9
"Love Song of J. Alfred
    Prufrock, The," 16–
    34

MacLeish, Archibald, 14,
    34, 57, 62, 109–10
Mallarmé, Stéphane, 101
Malte Laurids Brigge
    (Rilke), 18
Mann, Thomas, 29
Marlowe, Christopher, 84
Mechthild of Magdeburg,
    100
Mégroz, Rudolph L., 53
Meinong, Alexius, 9, 10, 11,
    102